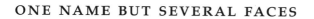

ONE NAME BUT SEVERAL FACES

GEORGIA SOUTHERN UNIVERSITY

JACK N. AND ADDIE D. AVERITT

LECTURE SERIES, NO. 5

VARIETY IN

· · · · · · · · ·

POPULAR

· · · · · · · · ·

CHRISTIAN

One
Name
but
Several
Faces

· · · · · · · · ·

DENOMINATIONS

· · · · · · · · ·

IN SOUTHERN

· · · · · · · · ·

HISTORY

Samuel S. Hill

THE UNIVERSITY OF GEORGIA PRESS : ATHENS AND LONDON

© 1996 by the University of Georgia Press
Athens, Georgia 30602
All rights reserved
Designed by Erin Kirk New
Set in 10 on 13 Palatino by Books International
Printed and bound by Thomson-Shore, Inc.

The paper in this book meets the guidelines for permanence
and durability of the Committee on Production Guidelines
for Book Longevity of the Council on Library Resources.

Printed in the United States of America

00   99   98   97   96   C   5   4   3   2   1

Library of Congress Cataloging in Publication Data

Hill, Samuel S.
    One name but several faces : variety in popular Christian
denominations in Southern history / Samuel S. Hill.
        p.   cm.
    Includes bibliographical references and index.
    ISBN 0-8203-1792-6 (alk. paper)
    1. Protestant churches—Southern States.   2. Southern
States—Church history.   I. Title.
BR535.H48   1996
280'.4'0975—dc20   95-20994

British Library Cataloging in Publication Data Available

FOR HELEN

Contents

Foreword

THE GEORGIA SOUTHERN UNIVERSITY academic community was deeply honored and challenged by the presence and
lectures of Dr. Samuel S. Hill on campus October 4–5, 1994.
The occasion was the fifth annual Jack N. and Addie D. Averitt
Lectures. Professor Hill's numerous books, articles, and lectures have long since earned him the reputation of being the
foremost living commentator and interpreter of religion in the
southern United States. His scholarly and prodding lectures
have now been expanded in this present volume without the
loss of their original appeal to those October listeners.

Professor Hill opens numerous doors by his creative explor-
ations in relation to pluralism (one name *can* have several
faces), freedom (which is expressed in dual directions—*from*
and *for*), creativity, and intensity in southern religion. Religion in the South is by no means a melting pot; it is Bruns-
wick stew! There is visible pluralism in the stew as well as a
unique flavor informed by freedom, creativity, and intensity.
With verve, alacrity, and his own unique creativity, Hill gives
the recipe for this southern dish of a select number of popular
Christian denominations in the South. He deftly tells the story
of religious pluralism in the South as illustrated by the various
Baptist bodies, the several "Christian" groups, and the some-

times overlooked "of God" or "Spirit movement" denominations.

Dr. Hill's first book, *Southern Churches in Crisis* (1966), had as one major purpose an examination of the "quality and potential of 'popular southern religion.'" Since then in his published works, he has examined in great depth the phenomenon of religion in the South and the role it has played in the lives of millions of people. By far his most expansive volume was his edited *Encyclopedia of Religion in the South* (1984). Even there his goal was the production of a "useful" volume rather than a "comprehensive" one. The area of "religion in the South" is far too large and complex to be explored completely even in a work of 864 pages, double columned!

The present lectures continue Hill's exploration of religion in the South in its popular dimension. No one in the academic setting would gainsay the role of the specialist in choosing special histories to tell. In limited lecture time and with pagination restraints, Professor Hill has chosen most appropriate groups in his presentation of the many faces of religion in the South, even among those groups that share names—"Baptists," "Christians," and "of God." No other work has explored these same name groups in the South more succinctly, clearly, and creatively. This volume can certainly help correct numerous misconceptions on the grassroots as well as academic levels concerning these "names" and "faces." In addition, Dr. Hill has given numerous and varied "pointers" for further research on religion in the South. Indeed, "the southern faithful's yearning for freedom"—rejecting, embracing, and enlarging—will continue to be creatively researched for many years to come, in large part due to Samuel S. Hill's prodding and challenging words in this volume and elsewhere.

Special appreciation "notes of thanks" must be sent in several directions. Dr. and Mrs. Averitt head the list, for without their generosity to scholarly pursuits there would have been no lectures nor published volumes. Other words of gratitude are extended to Walter J. Fraser, Jr., chair of the Department of

History, and to R. Frank Saunders, Jr., chair of the Averitt Lecture Committee. Fred Brogdon and Anastatia Sims also served effectively on this committee. Esther Mallard, coordinator of special collections, made important contributions to the committee. Peggy Smith, "super secretary" in the Department of History, did yeoman's service in relation to these lectures in a variety of ways. Malcolm Call, former director of the University of Georgia Press, gave valuable advice to the committee. In conclusion, to all those from the Georgia Southern community of learning, townspeople and out-of-townspeople, and special guests who responded so positively to the lectures and discussion during those two bright October days, a special card of thanks is extended.

GEORGE H. SHRIVER
AVERITT LECTURE COMMITTEE

Preface

THE INVITATION TO LECTURE at another university is an
honor much appreciated by an academician. But any such
kindness turns out to be far more than that. It becomes an
assignment to ponder what is in (if not yet on) one's mind
that one has not yet systematically addressed and formulated.
Scholarly work initiated in response to others' suppositions
that you have something "new" to say is different from course
teaching assignments or self-initiated projects. It really forces
one to stretch.

The faculty at Georgia Southern University accomplished
more than they knew—perhaps also less than they intended—
when they invited me to deliver the Jack N. and Addie D.
Averitt Lectures on 4–5 October, 1994. Already this young lec-
tureship has brought in scholars from whose work many of us
have profited. Accordingly, I rummaged around a bit to hit
upon a topic I hoped would prove of interest and value to students of the American South, especially students of the history
of its religious life.

A book's title can take only one subtitle. "Variety in Popular
Christian Denominations in Southern History" comes closest
to amplifying "One Name but Several Faces." A second subtitle, if allowed, would point to an important theme that runs

throughout these pages: the southern faithful's yearning for freedom. There are repeated instances of a passion to be free *from* constraints and restraints, and *for* the creativity to be authentic and effective in understanding the truth and practicing it.

In having to choose which Christian denominations to examine in whatever variety characterizes them, I decided on the Baptists, the "Christians," and the "of God" bodies. Treating the Baptists seemed unavoidable. There are millions of them and they are everywhere. The "Christians," with most attention devoted to the Restoration Movement that gave rise to the Christian Church (Disciples of Christ) and the Churches of Christ, have been significant in southern life for nearly two centuries. Nevertheless people are confused about who these groups are, a condition this book sets out to clarify. The "of God" bodies that came into being as the twentieth century dawned are heart and center of Pentecostalism. Confusion has been a problem in this case also; in addition many are mystified by the "speaking in tongues" phenomenon. Each chapter here is presented in hopes of supplanting darkness with light.

Whom have I to thank for beautiful hospitality on the campus of Georgia Southern and in the company of new and old friends there? More people than I can refer to by name, of course. But Frank Saunders, George and Cathy Shriver, Jay Fraser, and Peggy Smith hold especially warm places in my memory of that gratifying visit. Special gratitude goes out to Dr. and Mrs. Averitt without whom . . .

I intend for this text based on those lectures and all the stimulating discussion that followed them, to enhance the sponsoring institution and our understanding of this marvelous field of study, religion in the American South. May it be so.

ONE NAME BUT SEVERAL FACES

Introduction

THE AMERICAN RELIGIOUS SCENE has always been confusing to observers, both foreign and domestic. A major cause is
the enormous variety of names and titles used by Christian
groups. Even the American Jewish community is divided into
"denominations."

Quite recently this accustomed diversity has been expanded
to include other world religions now entrenched in American
society, Muslims, Buddhists, and Hindus, for example. Alas,
they too prove to be multiform. In some cases, members of one
sect of a major tradition will hardly recognize the teachings or
practices of another sect; in other cases, there may even be a
sense of betrayal or hostility felt by members of one group toward another. Sometimes a negative response results from the
charge that the adaptive or hybrid nature of a sect is as much
an American variant as it is the embodiment of an ancient heritage strong in India, China, Southeast Asia, the Middle East,
Africa, or elsewhere.

One is tempted to say "thank goodness for the South." In
one American region, anyway, the list is fairly short and a
name or title is readily recognizable. Alas and alack (*alas* is not
sufficient this time), so it used to be—for those who confined
their vision to the familiar or close to home, or to their own

social or racial configuration. If such simplicity and familiarity have ever been accurate, they are not any more. "Baptist" does not mean neatly "Baptist"; "Christian" cannot be taken at face value; "Pentecostal" is veritably bewildering.

Perhaps it took imports to shake up the domestic scene, to dislocate the taken-for-granted—imports referring not only to recently arrived or by now conspicuous religious groups from far away but also to nontraditional Western communities newly visible in the region, including Roman Catholics and classic evangelicals (a coinage to be described later).

Truth to tell, even Baptist, Methodist, and "Christian" have not been univocal namings in the region since the colonial period. Variety began early. Independent black Baptist churches date from the 1780s. Primitive (antimission) Baptists are found by some name and in some form by the earliest years of the nineteenth century. Free Will Baptists began emerging in the 1810s. Before 1845, white Baptists (other than Primitive and Free Will) belonged to a national, transregional fellowship, and then became a regional body, the Southern Baptist Convention. "Methodist" has been the identifier of black churches and white, of Republican Methodists and Methodist Protestants; not to mention the Methodist Episcopal Church, South that enjoyed great strength from 1844 to 1939—alongside the national (largely, though not totally, northern) Methodist Episcopal Church.

"Christian" likewise has designated, and continues to designate, more than one Christian grouping. The Republican Methodists changed their name (in 1793) to Christian Church after one year. Church leaders in New England who were to wield some influence on the South were aspiring to that simple appellation by the 1790s. Barton Warren Stone and his Kentucky and Ohio spiritual kinsmen were "Christians only" by 1805.

The time is ripe for students of the religious lives of southern people to investigate the varieties that have been generated. Actually in recent years more and more studies have pointed to diversity, long ago as well as on the current scene.[1]

This book undertakes to demonstrate such diversity by showing that one name can have several faces. The most salient significance of this acknowledgment has to do with how homogeneous the South's religious culture has been. In the early days of the discovery of southern religious history (between about 1964 and 1975), historians assumed a high degree of religious consensus.[2] Nearly everyone, it was thought, was a Baptist, Methodist, or Presbyterian, or held views quite similar to that large company. For example, "Baptist-like" was a term used to express strains on homogeneity in preference to speaking of heterogeneity. Moreover, each denominational title was presented as a homogeneous sector of the population.

One scholar who began early to challenge such generalizations and premises, Donald G. Mathews, has recently formulated his perspective this way. "The many denominational variations within traditions—such as those among pentecostals and Baptists of both races, for example—have not been adequately addressed." More pointedly he contends that "the fusion of these into reified things—Baptist, pentecostal—ignores the dynamism of southern religion." Pushing the argument farther by inverting it, he insists that the "assumption of division between such traditions" also ignored that dynamism.[3] Often simplicity has been detected where there was complexity, and division where there was unity. In total, Mathews's interpretation points to the fragility of the denominational units and their patterns for reliable research into southern religious history. *Fragility*, not uselessness or distortion.

This book predicates the utility, reliability, and authenticity of denominational patterns for effective research. But it seeks to avoid doing so provincially, not claiming too much for those data (really, that categorical datum). Mathews also calls for a truly sophisticated method and approach—which is beyond the scope of this inquiry (but deserves serious analysis). In his words: "We have assumed the homogeneity of southern religion without looking sufficiently at the nature of differences affected by class, music, region, and theological expression." Here the task is chiefly to ask some of the questions that lie beneath Mathews's large and rich design. Several possible lines for investigation follow.

What is the attraction of the titular names, terms, and words? Why has "Christian" or "of God" been chosen and held dear; why has it achieved acceptance across a spectrum?

Are the several bodies that go by one name kin to each other? If so, how; by theology and church practice? Or instead by a supinely clung-to familiar name? Or by race or class or region (or subregion)? Are the several versions of Baptists correlated in concentric circles? That is, do they have something in common with other name-sharers; is it not so much or quite a lot? Can they be first or third cousins rather than offspring of the same parents? Are the several "of God" groupings essentially unrelated, diverse expressions that go randomly by an available and chosen name? If the latter, wherein lies the allure of that name with little regard paid to its conscription by others? And what about sibling or cousinly bodies that do not refer to themselves by a kind of family name, that might as well be "Methodist" but are not.

Is the body indigenous or imported? If imported, how did its presence come to be a feature of southern life? Did regional transference alter its character—making it functionally indigenous despite foreign origination? As time has passed, has that community become observable only in the South, its ancestors either having moved away from where they started or having spawned a heritage that has not been able to sustain its initial impetus in a homeland elsewhere?

If the body is indigenous, what factors contributed most decisively to its origin? Did they pertain to dissension within an older body? If so, was that dissension grounded in theology mostly, or in church practices principally, or as a consequence of strife between leaders or cohorts of members bent on dominance or simply determined to have their own way?

Or did sectional differences and clashes prompt the indigeneity? Answering this last question takes up a considerable portion of this book. A telling critique from the Tennessee "Christian" leader, David Lipscomb, writing in 1891, provides a push:

> The southern Methodists are protesting against the tendency to reject the word of God by the Northern Methodists. Southern Presbyterians are objecting to the loose teachings of their Northern brethren. Baptists south are protesting against the setting aside of the word of God by their Northern brethren, and loose rationalistic and semi-infidel teachings are prevailing in some churches of Disciples in the northern states.[4]

What characterizes a particular name-grouping, as a whole or in its various parts? Is it continuity and stability or, alternatively, reaction and revolution? That is, is its (their) temperament to be mainstream and a contributor to civilization, or rather to stir things up by challenging conventions, religious and sociocultural? Has that temperament been multiple by stages? For example, were the "Christians" at one time concerned with stabilizing and perpetuating, only to take a different role for themselves in a later period? Are there some stabilizers and some revolters flying the same titular flag? What about the matter of cultural independence, to raise the same question in another way? Is the body willing in good conscience to read sociocultural needs, trends, and excitements as a guide toward formulating its vision and agenda? Or does it deliberately distance itself from what is popular and from people's perceptions of what is good and right or necessary and desirable because of a resolute commitment to a norm upheld as timeless?

Closely related to those inquiries is the issue, does a body undergo a shift in its social acceptance over time? Has it moved away from an early obscurity to a plane of high prominence? Or from marginality to integration, that is, to being an important participant in the general society and quite convinced that that is its calling? Or, as sometimes happens, has a religious group called off its truce with and its vital inclusion in general society for reasons of a calling to "come out," to stand in judgment both upon its sociocultural context and the "mother" denomination? If that seems contrary to the way things usually happen according to conventional wisdom, that is precisely correct. What the world thinks is no longer prized by people who think this way, the divine spirit having spoken and been allowed to have its way.

Is there a pattern of one becoming several? What began as a tightly united phalanx of soldiers in the Lord's army may discover grousing in the ranks and soon some splintering. As the group's life enlarges, so new leaders, new agendas, and new surrounding cultures create tensions leading to excrescences. Solidarity may give way to local interests or factionalism. Some fracturing of that kind may generate deep sorrow, but other instances reveal a defiant and imperious spirit.

Did the frontier contribute to a body's formation, or later to a transformation of its mission, clientele, and degree of social inclusion? Did the Civil War and sectionalist values and factions that led up to it play a part? What about urbanization and industrialization, people's moving from farming to wages employment—the modernization and rationalization of living; was this tension-producing passage an occasion for a fresh creativity? Similarly, what about new currents of thought, new ways of thinking, among them Baconian or Darwinian developments in science with modes, metaphors, and paradigms that were borrowed and adapted by general culture and church culture? Have the emergent perspectives and methods in the humanities and social sciences—historicism, textual criticism, psychology, and sociology, to cite only a few—compelled reconsideration of religious assumptions long in place and held irrevocable?

A final issue of keen importance has to do with timing. What conditions surrounded a religious group's coming to birth, or a major shift in its understanding as to its responsibility toward society, or its hiving off into two or more sects? In the South's history, have there been particularly fecund periods for formation, for flourishing, for conflict, or even for decline?

With this list of issues in mind, this book treats three name-groupings common in the American South. First is the Baptist, the subject of chapter 1. Everyone knows that this is much the largest Christian denomination (a word that means "naming") in the region. Any study of the selected topic does well to include this massive company of Protestant Christians, numbering at least 25 million in the region. The task here is to describe some of the variety within that company along two lines: (1) demonstrating its complexity by reporting on this, that, and the other kind of Baptists, and (2) working to account both for the process of diversification and for the empirical forms that process has given rise to. No one body of Baptists receives exhaustive treatment, several are merely mentioned, and many are omitted. Even a brief cataloging, however, should exemplify the Baptist diversity and the multiple religious, historical, and cultural factors that have made that grouping what it is, as a name-unit and by numerous subparts.

Chapter 2 is all about the "Christians." This topic possesses special appeal, indeed suggests some intrigue, because Christian and "Christian" seem to constitute either redundancy or confrontation. Why would any group claim for itself an entitlement that all followers of Christ have always used casually and appropriately simply to identify themselves? The "Christian" phenomenon, associated with the Restoration Movement of the nineteenth century for the largest part, was surely getting at something fresh or distinctive—actually "ancient" in its own understanding. Those who discovered that title ("Christian") were certain that a new historical era had dawned. All previous Christian movements were somehow lacking, though not necessarily regarded as heretical or inauthentic. The timing issue would seem to be uniquely important when applied to this case.

"Of God" Christian bodies are title and substance of the analysis in chapter 3. "Church of God," sometimes with an additional suffix, is a straightforward name. Yet, as with consideration of "Christian" bodies, one is prompted to inquire into why the existing communities of the Christian faithful, some centuries old, were not people of the Church of God, or at least of God's church. In this case, too, something is going on; a new revelation has been received; and a new conception has arisen of what the truest church should be. Incidentally, in chapter 3 I use "Church of God" and "Spirit Movement" almost interchangeably since not all groupings of the genre have chosen the "of God" title. The genre may quite accurately be referred to as Spirit Movement since direct and overpowering outpourings of the Holy Spirit are characteristic. Also virtually all—one never says *all* when classifying religious bodies—"of God" denominations popular in the South are Pentecostal.

Other name-groupings could have been chosen, of course. Methodist loomed as an appealing candidate since several distinct bodies stand in that Protestant tradition. Roman Catholic did not, inasmuch as there are no official subdivisions of that Church; also historically it has been weak in the South. Lutheran, Episcopal, and Presbyterian might have been selected but none offers great diversity in the region, and the first is quite small. Moreover all are historic European communions emanating from the Protestant Reformation and therefore not, in any sense, native to regional culture.

Baptist, "Christian," and "of God" (or Spirit Movement) prevailed in the competition for three principal reasons. First, they are large and widely distributed families. Second, all have occasioned some births, some beginnings, and some indigenous formations in the South. Third, their lives in the regional culture afford transparency to many of the received traditions, currents of thought, transitions, and transformations in the South's history from 1750 forward, but especially in the nineteenth century. Baptist, "Christian," and "of God" communities, in their variety, are presented, seriatim, one chapter describing each.

Concurrently the flow of the analysis will display cumulative aspects. Chapter 1 on the Baptist denomination will anticipate some of the analysis to take place in 2 and 3. Chapter 3 on the "of God" bodies will reap some benefit and direction from the two previous treatments. And so on. Throughout, this book aims to see each community on its own terms and, in addition, to compare. Comparison between and among the three denominations will, according to design, illuminate each. Chronological, contextual, and theological dimensions are elementary to the study of each and all together.

The historical framework treated the most fully here is the nineteenth century. But of course there is overlap with the preceding and following time units we artificially call centuries. Events in Baptist history in the eighteenth century are elemental for the stories told here. Developments to 1920 or so are integral to the "of God" movements that really began in the 1880s and 1890s.

The sharpest focus is on the three name-groups, the variety within them, and their place in the history of the South. Yet the themes of freedom and creativity are threads appearing throughout. At one basic level all three were part and parcel of the new nation's quest for a satisfactory identity; in the process, religious people availed themselves of the luxury of being free. All were sloughing off old patterns, conventions, and constraints that did not fit either their faith convictions or their sociocultural situations. Repeatedly they struggled with those features of their living and wrought creatively to respond to them. The several Baptist, "Christian," and "of God" communities that emerged or underwent adaptation manifested courage, imagination, and persistence. Their stories are impressive, occasioning more than a little admiration and inspiration.

ANY REAL ACQUAINTANCE with southern religious history equips a person with the knowledge that the evangelical family of Protestant Christianity has long been the region's largest and most influential heritage. So much so that for the first decade or two of the scholarly study of this subject, commencing in the 1960s, the theme of evangelical dominance shaped the work done. More recent historiography has taken into account the variety of religious forms and forces that have been part of the region's religious history. This book aims to correlate those two scholarly perspectives. Put another way, I examine subsets within sets, species within genres, and this and that collection of Baptists within the larger Baptist community; similarly the "Christians" and the "of God" people.

With only a little reflection, we all realize how important names are; what people call themselves is deeply significant. Even the most poised person does not enjoy being mistakenly referred to or having her name mispronounced or misspelled. Few things in life are more axiomatic than the congruity between you and your name. It is not excessive by much to say, "I am my name."

Christian denominations attach almost that much significance to their namings. Several subsets in the three groupings under consideration here are acutely convinced of their special destiny; they insist in particular on being nominated for what they are. Many "Christians" can hardly imagine how any disciple of Christ can subvert that naming for anything else. Or why would anyone want to? The same applies to the people in an "of God" body, notably any Church of God fellowship, since that phrase is common in the New Testament. One hears them say, "We just call ourselves what the early Christians called themselves." Baptists, too, relish the sound of their denominational name without, however, making an ontological claim for its propriety; perhaps for their own subset, but not for the name. In the South, the Baptist disposition would seem to be more cultural than biblical or theological, especially in areas where the numerical predominance of Baptists may tempt some degree of a triumphalist spirit.

As it happens, all three of these popular denominations participate in the Protestant family called *evangelical*, or at least have some historical relation to it. In any Protestant taxonomy, where else could you place the "of God" bodies (varied as they are)? Similarly the Baptists. Yet, precisely because name and lineage are matters of such significance, Baptists manifest a certain aversion to classification. Many hump their backs slightly at being thought of as "evangelical" and even stiffen them in insisting that they are not "Protestant." "Christians" often have been positioned under the evangelical heading, but none really feel at home in that family. Just the same, the "Christians" do have some historical affinity to evangelical sensibilities. All of those descriptions must, and will, receive some attention in this book; and the entire subject is bound up with the cultural history of the South.

What does it mean to be evangelical? First, evangelical Christians are authority-minded, live with a keen sense of personal answerability and accountability, and are impelled by a mission to other people, as individuals and as communities. If they seem to know more about ultimate being and truth than others, it is because God chooses to be so accessible to them in offering himself to human experience and revealing truth reliably, perhaps even inerrantly. Taken as a whole and highlighted, evangelical Christianity stresses authority, personal accountability, and mission to the world.

Turning earthy, one may speak of evangelicals as a hungry and thirsty people. They want to know God himself and truth itself fully, informingly. They are induced to such craving by the assurance that the personal God is accessible and his truth definitively clear. "A theology of unmediated encounter" is a common depiction of the evangelical understanding. At least in some of its forms, evangelicalism appears to render the Bible an extension of divinity or to regard personal religious experience as all but overpowering human frailty and limitation— both toward dispelling mystery and collapsing the transcendent and immanent realms into one. Always evangelicals intimately know the Lord and authoritatively know the truth he reveals.

All who have paid close attention to the popular religion of the American South will recognize some of the traits that this description intends to capture. This characterization refers to the American evangelical tradition in general and lacks 100 percent applicability to southern forms of that family. First, the South is not headquarters area of American evangelicalism; southern Michigan west to St. Paul may be. Second, northern evangelicalism stands closer to the classical tradition, in which comprehensive witness and systematic thinking prevail. Distinctive southern features include: (1) the disinterest on the part of the largest Baptist denominations, black and white, in joining the National Association of Evangelicals; (2) the general absence of disciplined spirituality in southern forms; (3) a comparatively small interest in taking radical ethical positions; and (4) a far greater preference for "conversionist" than "confessionalist" orientation; that is, the southern forms are more active than they are reflective.

The evangelical temperament, irrespective of locale and era, acknowledges nothing in history as norm*al*. Norm*ative* is basic, basic, basic. Since nothing "here on earth below" corresponds to God's perfection, Christians must be vigilant, ever on the alert, to contend with sin in living and with heresy and sloth in the church. Because of their intensity over these concerns, disease, reform, and schism are predictable courses of behavior. It is not surprising that these religious springs of action issue in the formation of multiple kinds of Baptists, "Christians," and "of God" bodies. Evangelicals never get enough of purity, authenticity, and normativity. It is their nature to be restless, never quite to "settle in." One could say much the same thing about the entire Protestant heritage, emphatically for its first century. But it was the Baptist element in that stream that, more than any other, continued to be driven by restlessness, by "never getting enough of." That restlessness with Baptist coloration made an indelible imprint on southern culture. But the two other popular denominations, the "Christians" and the "of God" people, are simply younger cousins of the traditional Baptists. In fact, Baptist influence, direct and indirect, was one of the creative forces that helped midwife the birth of those two bodies.

The setting was the American South, especially its nineteenth-century history. Southerners were caught in the throes of modern changes—political, economic, social, and religious; accordingly they adjusted, adapted, defended, created, struck off on innovative courses, and accommodated. There was some real genius (also much perversity) in the cases they made for slavery and in the promotion of the South's superiority, to cite two instances. Southern literacy rates may have been low and the capacity for fantasizing high, but minds and spirits were at work. That is evident in the emergent religious formations within the three groups and some others as well. There may have been an angry and reactionary spirit in splintering, but there was also creativity.

What resources and concerns do these religious legacies and the conditions of the nineteenth-century South share that give impetus to several new creations and such impressive creativity? The answer is freedom. Freedom's expressions were variously blind, provincial, perverse, generative, constructive, effective, and admirable. In the religious area, research reveals numerous yearnings for freedom, always a freedom *from* something and *for* something. The four freedoms listed below cluster a larger number of freedom concerns, which animated southerners' religious lives in that century and led to the new formations.

1. Freedom from domination by social class, tradition, or both, eighteenth-century Virginia developments being a prime example;
2. from church, theological system, or both, the Stone-Campbell "Christian" movement, for example;
3. from denial of the right to "our own religious life," the experience of post-Emancipation black people bulking huge; and

4. from the constraints of polite society's conventionality, revivalists and pentecostalists being obvious referents.

Readers familiar with Nathan Hatch's 1989 book, *The Democratization of American Christianity*, at once recognize that these developments have some, often much, in common with the general American history of the period.[5] Perhaps some will think back to the first time they realized that the Mason–Dixon line and the northern boundaries of the Confederate States of America, all things considered, really were artificial. As regional as these developments were, they were also influenced by what was taking place elsewhere in the country, and they paralleled similar quests for freedom and authenticity that have characterized American religious history.

CHAPTER 1

The Baptists

THE PROTESTANT RADICALS called Baptists were in the South early and from the first decades were diverse. This branch of English reform and dissent had appeared about 1610, its constituents classic exemplars of the evangelical principle described as "restless," "never having enough," "always taking stock," never quite "settling in." Indeed an old and still apt characterization of the Baptists is that they simply wanted to take the Protestant Reformation to its logical conclusion. Reliance on the Bible and devotion to the God known directly in personal experience (variously interpreted) is what they stood for. Other post-Reformation Christians, their spiritual brothers and sisters, had stopped short. These people were hearing the divine calling to embody full Christian belief and discipleship.

Baptistism is not inherently a connectional system. The implication of this aspect of that denomination's life, the ease with which division can occur, and even the tendency to divide, has been apparent among the Baptists of the South throughout their history. These Christians cluster in congregations; they are not isolates, or a go-it-alone kind of people. But the company they most like to keep is the local congregation. They *may* do more, associate more widely, but at local option. Historically a major issue of contention is precisely that: Is each local unit ultimate, or should it, does it relinquish some of its control by joining hands—and projects—with like-minded local units? All are agreed, no matter what their answer, that no institutional, earthly authority has jurisdiction over that quintessential Baptist collectivity, the local congregation. Thus an association of neighboring Baptist churches is an entity different in quantity and quality from Methodist conferences, Presbyterian synods, or Episcopal dioceses. A wider organization, a Baptist state convention, holds similarly curtailed powers, in fact no real power at all. Throughout this system, any and all agreements to associating are voluntary, and the agreements are informal, less than contractual. A congregation can choose to remain unaffiliated or to withdraw from an affiliation earlier entered into. It is also subject to dismissal from the larger grouping. The voluntary principle prevails.

That local-autonomy feature of Baptist life is a major source of its diversity (informal as well as official). It is one feature among many that has made these people at home in the American South. For the Baptists, dissent, self-assertion, reform, and building new organizations have been standard behavior. Freedom, creative religious freedom, is a commonplace in the region's religious history. The Baptist presence in the region has helped foster that freedom and has even exacerbated the issues and problems associated with it.

It is inviting, if quite provincial, to think of the Southern Baptist Convention when considering the subject of Baptists in the American South. Two main fallacies inhabit such thinking: (1) there are scores of kinds of Baptists, and in many cases they resemble each other little and have nothing to do with each other; (2) the Southern Baptist Convention is itself highly diverse. I begin with the second point.

Historian Walter B. Shurden has pointed out the reality and impact of four distinct subtraditions within that 15-million-member communion. He calls them the Charleston Tradition, the Sandy Creek, the Georgia, and the Tennessee. First manifestations of the four appeared, respectively, in the 1690s, the 1750s, the 1840s, and the 1850s. (The earlier two are more precisely datable than the ones expansively titled *Georgia* and *Tennessee*.)[1] Shurden seeks to characterize them as, in sequence, concerned with "order," "ardor," "cultural identity," and "ecclesiastical identity." Even if one were to challenge aspects of his formulation, one can readily grant that the four character traits inform the larger heritage—and that they came from somewhere.

The Charleston Tradition began when a colony of Baptists, not long removed from England, moved far down the coast from New Hampshire and Maine. Their roots lay in Particular Baptist thought, Particular referring to Calvinist sentiments. Their believing was pointed and substantial. Of course, being Baptists they had known something of God directly in their own hearts. But the rule of their sole authority, Holy Scripture, was primary. Shurden nicknames them semi-Presbyterians owing to their tastes and convictions concerning order. For this kind of a Baptist, everything a congregation does should be orderly, within bounds, definitely purposive. Thus they practiced ecclesiastical order—effective congregational governance; liturgical order—their worship was planned and dignified; and ministerial order—the clergy would live up to high standards of preparedness and personal demeanor. Almost inevitably a Baptist life so structured (ordered) implies connectedness with other congregations. Still, what one local unit wants for itself and thinks of itself takes second place to doing things right and well. Strident isolation does not emanate from such a perspective.

The Sandy Creek Tradition is a "whole 'nother thing." These Baptists were zealots, establishment-rejecters, and respecters of convention and propriety little if at all; rarely were they viewed as respectable people. Arising from the New Light sentiment that speckled New England's radical fringe of Congregationalists and Presbyterians as well as Baptists, these Separate Baptists formed a congregation near Greensboro, North Carolina, in 1755. The Sandy Creek Church was very rural indeed in the setting of truly frontier conditions.[2]

As their name, Separate Baptists, suggests, they were neither semi-Presbyterian nor connectionalist. The church as a body was less important to them than the true-hearted, transformed individuals comprising it. They employed that season's "new measure," revivalism in an early form; they aggressively strove to capitalize on effective means for the instant and datable conversion experience, often in an emotion-charged context. This became the revivalistic tradition. It is important to note that not all Southern Baptists have always been, or are, evangelistic according to the revivalistic mode. Charleston's *order* produces quite another kind of Christian and congregation from Sandy Creek's *ardor*, although many have had it both ways, inconsistent as such a pairing may seem.

Georgia Tradition is the heading Shurden gives to the cultural-identity element so powerful in the Southern Baptist Convention, even though symbolism is more important than place in this construction. Between 1845 and 1870 two major impulses came to life. In the earlier year, the convention itself was organized, in Augusta. Under strain for some time, the old Triennial Convention of Baptists, formed in 1814 and national in scope, came apart. Sectionalism-related causes were the largest part of the story. Whether it was permissible for ministers, or secondarily lay people, to own slaves arose as a sharply contested point. A second factor contributed to the breakup as well: the trend that had been developing in the South toward forming a more centralized denominational structure. Thus in 1845 when the division was fully acknowledged at the Augusta meeting, it was a convention with boards and agencies under the governance of the whole body that appeared. In the North for decades thereafter, the pattern of more independent boards and agencies persisted. The rudiments of the Southern Convention's first region-serving board date from the work of I. T. Tichenor in "home missions" operating from Atlanta in the late 1860s. Before the Civil War, the regional body arose; after it, agencies such as Tichenor's home mission board arose, serving the region through the support of the organized denominational fellowship. Connectionalism had arrived in substantial force; the place of that development in regional religious history is a major story.

By historic Baptist lights, the Tennessee Tradition is a curious one, the more so because of its claims about history. Calling themselves Landmark Baptists, these people posited an unbroken succession from New Testament times to every subsequent present time through Baptist or quasi-Baptist people and beliefs. The fellow Tennesseans of founder James R. Graves (born in Vermont), the "Christians" (later called Churches of Christ) also were concerned with the history of God's truth from the primitive age to the present. Their tack was restoration; but the Landmark Baptists saw an unbroken succession of the true church. They regarded that succession as necessary to legitimate the local Baptist congregation which, they dogmatized, is the only real church. By definition, ecclesiological authenticity entailed "Baptist," "local," and "in historical succession." All other "churches" are impostors, including malconstituted Baptist ones. Here then is a major source of exclusivism, sectarianism, or antiecumenical spirit in Southern Baptist Convention life.

Order, ardor, cultural identity, and ecclesiastical identity, according to Shurden's perceptive interpretation, are the constituent streams in the thinking of Southern Baptist Convention people. That would mean, if any person or congregation embodied them all that the mix would contain dignity and propriety; fervor and urgency; a keen sense of being a Southern Baptist—not merely a Baptist in the South or a plain Baptist; and a conviction of the exclusive correctness of this Christian perspective. In actuality, no one person can embody them all, and probably no single congregation can accommodate them all, not for long, at any rate. But those features, inclinations, and convictions are all present, and they all exert influence on ministers, lay leaders, and congregation members alike.

Historically, the formation of these four qualities dates from the period of founding before 1700, the coming of age of the frontier society around 1760, the tightening of regional cultural awareness, and the separation of the pure in mind from the surrounding culture and other Christian forms. Geographically, the four emerge farther west as stages pass: from New England–derived coastal Carolina; to the frontier east and then west of the mountains; to the Deep South where "the South" as a political and social culture takes shape; to the incipient western frontier where competition and swagger obtain. (Glancing at the recent past offers insight into why the Southern Baptist Convention has suffered such severe conflict since about 1975. Acknowledging this four-part heritage causes one to wonder how the body remained intact, effectively united, for so long.) The potential for division, whether informal or institutionally profound, always loomed. Perhaps it was the demise of the southern region, threatened or largely realized, that occasioned the transition from simple diversity to harsh polarization. The Georgia Tradition, it would seem plausible to contend, provided the glue that held together old English Baptistism (Charleston) and new American revivalistic evangelicalism (Sandy Creek). Once the cultural foundation became fragile, the spirit of exclusive authenticity (Tennessee) wrought its effective work.

The diversity is great. It always has been—at least since the Great Awakening era of the third quarter of the eighteenth century. Given the Baptist practice of local congregational autonomy, even when it is imperfectly lived out, uniformity never has characterized the tradition. Baptist life in the South had taken two of its four classic forms before the close of the colonial period and within the first sixty years of that denomination's debut in the region. Even so, by the generation in which the Republic was founded, most varieties of Baptist life had not yet appeared. To that date, there were few African Americans converted to Christianity in general or specifically to the Baptist faith. Yet to appear were the black churches and black denominations, and of course the Landmarkists. The same applies to others, too, Primitive Baptists and Fundamentalist Baptists among them. Tracking this evolution and these emergences is risk filled at best. But the attempt may provide some kind of mapping, or a time-line, on a subject a good deal more fascinating and significant than a puzzled outsider might have supposed.

Baptists in the South began as heirs of English Baptists who had settled in the coastal areas of northern New England then moved to the coastal areas of southern Carolina and to Tidewater Virginia south of the James River. They proved moderately effective in establishing congregations on the lower Atlantic seaboard from as far south as Charleston northward to the Norfolk-Portsmouth area.[3]

As Baptist ranks swelled in the Middle Atlantic and New England states, an adapting form of England-originated Baptist life emerged, more Calvinist than Arminian; a mixture of election and free-will doctrine became the influential element in the denomination. The Philadelphia Baptist Association was formed in 1707. It served as a link, a kind of coordinating agency, between members from the New England states and New York through the middle colonies and down to Maryland and Virginia. Through this loose-knit cooperative undertaking, mission efforts were undertaken, not yet overseas of course, but in planting churches and serving human needs. As the decades passed, publishing and educational efforts attracted support from these informally allied Baptists and resulted in advancing Christian civilization. A very low-key form of connectionalism this was, but it foretold the convictions of most North American Baptists that local congregations, while "autonomous," did not exist in isolation. Neither were they radical sectarians, meaning that they did participate in the public life of their times. Some, and a sizable minority all along, have taken exception to that posture and have withdrawn in the interest of purity.

By the middle of the eighteenth century, Baptist people and influence were found here and there, in town and rural areas. They were a presence to be noted, were increasingly taken quite seriously since they had graduated from a more self-contained, sometimes defiant, community to one with tentacles beyond their own membership and a more mainstream social position. Yet they were still Baptists, meaning that they swore no allegiance to any human authority, ecclesiastical or political, often displaying courage or a testy spirit.

No one was more of a Baptist in this resolute, testy manner than John Leland. A New Englander by birth and residence for most of his life, Leland moved to Virginia for the period 1777 to 1791 and is a legendary figure to all who cherish strong convictions about "separation of church and state." His encouragement to Baptist preachers fighting to topple Virginia's church Establishment bolstered their willingness to go to jail in defense of religious liberty. His voice and pen were part of the stream of Madisonian and Jeffersonian assaults on European-style state support for a society's designated church. To Leland's mind, the ontological priority lay with individuals, not the society. He went so far as to declare government a necessary evil. In 1815–16, Leland was a prominent spokesman in the cause of stopping mail transportation on Sunday. Not even government offering a desired service to the citizens should be allowed to contravene Sabbath observance, just as individuals take priority over society. God has priority over all human actions and institutions. Leland had strong convictions about the institutionalization of religion, too; he stood foursquare against all "extracongregational institutions," (another instance of the freedom issue central to the treatment in this book).[4]

But other currents were stirring among New England Protestants as New Lights appeared in Congregational, Presbyterian, and Baptist churches. In classic analytic terms this unrest, often more like an upheaval, may be referred to as revitalization. Recall the persistent sentiment among the kinds of Protestants I am discussing: they never quite settle in; they never get enough of purity, authenticity, and normativity. By the standards of the time, they were indeed radical. They had it in for the old system, the standing order, and any version of establishment.

What they insisted on was "overthrow"; reform did not go nearly far enough. Baptists in the Northeast were affected by the Great Awakening of 1730–50; those whose vitalistic sensibilities were inflamed craved renewal. Regarding mere correct belief and earnest practice as good but insufficient, they promoted intense, zealous, emotional religious experience.

Such Christians are active and determined. They are busy in their own communities. But Christ's commission knows no boundaries. As if to demonstrate that principle, in 1754 a small band left upstate Connecticut to evangelize the South. After a brief residence near Winchester, Virginia, they found their Zion in central North Carolina. Their accomplishments there, especially longer term, far surpassed what the movement had wrought at home. Soon they were everywhere, it seemed, converting, revitalizing, and starting new Separate Baptist churches. Not much came of the first congregation at Sandy Creek, but these devout souls founded an association of churches by that name, and they evangelized far and wide, from Virginia to Georgia. In seventeen years they planted forty-two churches and generated a preacher roster that soared to 125.[5] One major sector, and certainly the stereotype, of Southern Baptists traces to this rootage; its actual character has ever since reflected the evangelism-through-revivalism that this movement launched.

One does not need to strain to suppose that these Separate Baptists, so different from the Tidewater Baptists of England and New England descent, met with little social acceptance. The truth is that they craved even less than they got. The plaudits of other people concerned them scarcely at all. But it was their spirit, in a peculiar sort of league with the tough-minded, less emotional, religious-liberty-loving Baptist "fanatics," that went so far toward overturning accustomed Virginia folkways, standards of proper decorum, and even the forms of governing the society. Maybe the bottom rail was not on the top this early, but the plain folks, yeoman farmers and small merchants, redirected the course of society. Among other effects, the manners of the gentry and the lifelessness of the churches were transformed. Increasingly, standing and authority were not privileges one was born to, but positions deserving and self-asserting people rose to, in reality, took for themselves. These rugged, sometimes crude Baptists, some heart driven, others impelled by their thinking on the nature of society, played a major role in transforming a hierarchical society into a popular one.[6]

These Separates semiofficially joined forces with the Regular Baptists in 1801 in Kentucky, the new spiritual hotbed in the West. However, *joining with* must not be taken to mean that their modes and mentalities were absorbed. Their revivalistic heritage persisted and remains powerful to our own times. Indeed, in the nineteenth century their style of evangelism was a hallmark of Baptist life, more nearly exclusively south and west of Virginia and the Carolinas than in those three states, but everywhere.

Most of the Baptists of Separate heritage blended into the enlarging, eventually massive company of Southern Baptists. Certainly their special form of evangelism persisted and penetrated forever the life of this community of faith. That form and force was itself a creative invention and one that the Southern Baptists have revised and perfected. There is probably more continuity between the Separates' theology and techniques—which initially they shared with other New Lights—and later American approaches to revivalism than in any other evangelistic tradition. These Baptists of the South were about the business of saving souls before the Great Revival on the western frontier and the modern revivalism that has passed from Charles G. Finney to Dwight L. Moody and Billy Sunday to Billy Graham. This one (regional) denomination has retained, and enlarged, this device straight through from the middle of the eighteenth century. Other revivalistic forms have either arisen later or been set aside in favor of other emphases and approaches. The Separate Baptists' heritage that made the worship occasion mostly a means to the end of bringing about conversion has been so powerful that that purpose essentially supplanted worship as the expression of congregational gatherings.

But some Separates held fast, resisting the blandishments of cooperation, organization, and subscription to stated doctrinal standards. They even condemned the rather mild Philadelphia Confession, a compendium of Baptist beliefs drawn up in 1742. The Bible alone; no creeds, no confessions. Their feelings ran deep. The uneasy alliance of Separates and Regulars in Kentucky in 1801 witnessed minority defection two years later. Most of this radical band were attracted to the Stone-Campbell movement of Restoration-bent "Christians" (see chapter 2). The Stoneite wing of that movement was particularly attractive to them. For one thing, it was present and accessible in their new homelands of Kentucky and Tennessee. (The Campbell subtradition had not yet emerged and was not to make much impact in the western border areas until the 1820s.) For another, Stone and his followers were commendably anti-institutional, both with respect to creeds and to organized activities. This is not the only case of "switching" in the denominational history of southern Protestant people in the early national period. In those days, as in our own time, other matters may outrank membership in a particular body known by a given name. One would rather be right than a ———. Then, the drive toward freedom from any kind of authority or control predominated.

On seemingly all fronts, the Baptists were consolidating and expanding. Their success stories are impressive: in winning converts and starting churches; in organizing local associations and state conventions for cooperative endeavors, especially missions; in establishing publishing houses and academies and colleges. Two lineaments of this quite large-scale development are especially noteworthy. Baptists in the South worked in concert with Baptists to the north in the Triennial Convention in missionary, publishing, and educational work with enthusiasm from 1814 into the early 1830s. But sectional spirit and walls were building; and the entire national, interregional enterprise came apart officially in 1845 with the founding of the Southern Baptist Convention. The second development was the trend toward centralization and away from strictly local governance. One by one, state conventions emerged; for progressive Baptists, cooperative efforts and effective planning execution became the better way to do the Lord's bidding. They had no doubt that they could do many tasks better in league with others than by themselves. And in this era of consolidation and expansion in national society, they dedicated themselves to those heavenly commissions, winning the world to Christ and building a Christian civilization.

But not all the Baptists in the South were "progressive." Turning modern, rationalizing churches' work was no virtue at all to a small but forceful cadre that was emerging by 1810 or 1815. They were the antimission Baptists, some of whom called themselves Primitive Baptists, or Hard Shell or Old School Baptists. They developed the greatest strength usually in rural, socially cohesive areas, among them Maryland, eastern North Carolina, central Kentucky, and west Tennessee. A strict Calvinist theology, not a practical or functional one, informed their perspective on the churches' mission. Some with a propensity for what is modern might go so far as to doubt that Calvinism had appeal, but the antimission Baptists were hot-blooded Calvinists by deepest conviction. They firmly believed that God would accomplish his ends in his own way and time; otherwise, horror of horrors, his governance of the world would be left to the hands of free-willing depraved humanity.[7]

One of the arresting subthemes in the early Baptist story is its interregionality and interdenominationality. Even the Primitive Baptists, who were dedicated to localism and censorious of organized cooperative efforts, participated in those activities. The two earliest leaders of this stratum of Baptists were the New Englanders Abner Jones and Elias Smith, whom the subsequent "Christians" (of the Stone-Campbell heritage) were to claim as antecedent kinsmen, if not quite full-fledged brothers in the true church. From 1802 forward, Jones and Smith were seeing the same light as the Stoneites were soon to do and, a bit later, the southern Primitives. Their respective careers as Baptists did not last long, however; the two men retreated to a community of the like-minded who after 1820 were called the "Christian Connection." (The Jones-Smith stratum of Baptists receives further attention in chapter 2).

In this setting it is informative to observe that New Englanders and Baptists who turned "Christians" aligned themselves in ways that Primitive Baptists and Stoneites could admire. They embodied what historian Byron C. Lambert has described as "one expression of the American doctrine of freedom." They were early advocates of congregational autonomy that resisted any intercongregational organization. To Elias Smith, missionary societies "were but one phase of a wider movement to divest Americans of their liberties." A strong accusation that is, and one sincerely held. Liberty, equality, and righteousness were all consistent with and demanded by the Lord in heaven. Going further, Smith showed the value he attached to the new nation in continuing that "it is from heaven. . . . The establishment of the [American] government was an earnest of the final reign of Christ." The Stoneites and the Primitive Baptists took exception to his exaltation of America to so lofty a height, but they shared his condemnation of societies and interchurch cooperative agencies.[8]

These antimission sentiments were carried west by Primitive Baptists Daniel Parker and John Taylor, among others. There, under malleable and not yet tainted sociopolitical conditions, they held on to their freedom and sought to live a natural (in the state of nature) life. They opposed the newfangled (and certainly unbiblical) practices of an educated ministry, ornamented church buildings, instrumental music, and organized mission societies. Daniel Parker of Virginia, who moved to Tennessee in 1803 and on to southeast Illinois in 1816, clinched the point by drawing on the case of Jonah in the Old Testament. That prophet was called and sent directly by God, he had no seminary education; no society employed him; and he depended on no funds for support. The divergence between the organizing Baptists and the antimission Baptists was so sharp as to make one question whether they really warranted being referred to by the same name.

The Primitive Baptists represented another force surfacing in the Old South: namely, resistance to man-made, newfangled devices for performing service to the transcendent God. They regarded these organized cooperative undertakings as a "new thing." Promoters of such plans they accused of seeking "respectability," desirous of being "like other people," presumptuous toward "helping the Almighty carry on his own work." As one report from eastern North Carolina's Kehukee Baptist Association put it: any such activity is "worldly in character and insulting in its nature to the King of Zion." As if to clinch the point, the Kehukeeites derided their fellow Baptists, the cooperating sorts, as being as bad as Methodists, Presbyterians, Episcopalians, Quakers, Campbellites, or Catholics.[9]

This resistance theme is also reflected in the "Christians" and the "of God" bodies. "Restoration of the ancient order" and "restoration of the apostolic faith" are the slogans they respectively rallied to. A kinship does exist between these Primitive Baptists and the other groups. Antimission by conviction, the Primitives knew they had latched on to something. The Bible, they were certain, was on their side; more properly, they were on its side. Second, a treacherous full tide of bourgeois values was about to swamp the historic church. These devout would have none of it. By 1844 that holy company had grown to some 68,000 members, 900 ministers, and 1,622 churches.[10] The Primitive Baptists were on the map. Various spiritual kinsmen, with whom they had nothing to do of course, were taking the same intransigent stand beneath other denominational banners. Incidentally, the Primitive Baptists were antimission only in a certain sense. They did not oppose a person going out to serve as a missionary. They took their stand against institutionalization, against treating evangelism as a commodity, and against people being paid for such service.[11]

Initially the Primitives' direct opposition was to mission organizations and activities among people near by. But after 1814, an overseas enterprise was building, through the transregional Triennial Convention. More of the foreign mission efforts emanated in the North than in the South. Their appointees in this era went out to Burma and India, in the main. (Those mission fields remain the concentration of northern Baptist work [the American Baptist Churches, U.S.A.]; they have never been locales of Southern Baptist Convention overseas ministries.) According to the most reliable estimates, about two hundred foreign missionaries had been commissioned by 1845, most of them from the northern states.

IF THE PRIMITIVE BAPTISTS were revolutionary in seeking authenticity, which they understood to mean a pure faithfulness to the Bible and resisting all siren calls from worldly attachments, another dissident sector aimed to radically reform the Baptist churches, that is, to divert them from their errant paths to the straight and narrow. These were the Landmarkists who went to the extreme of denying the Christian legitimacy of all others than Baptists, and even of many Baptists. Their position was so strident that their existence tended to be either deified or damned. What most others then and later have judged to be exclusivism and an obnoxious triumphalism, the Landmarkists knew to be sound biblicism and good history.

What was the heart of the Landmark program? The only true churches are local Baptist churches. How did they know this to be true? Their claim rests in part on a constitutionalist view of the New Testament; there the perfect makeup of a church, qualified members and authorized office-holders, is plainly laid out. It also rests on the perpetuation of that primitive essence in pure churches across the intervening centuries. Everything but Baptist and quasi-Baptist churches has been an aberration and perversion, they contend. In the divine design, these true communities enjoyed an unbroken succession in the Mediterranean countries and other European societies until Baptists, by that identification, emerged in the early seventeenth century. But Baptists did not *emerge*; they had been present in history all along. Only the identification by that name was novel.[12]

In the 1840s James R. Graves, a Vermonter moved to Tennessee, began heralding this Landmarkist admixture of biblicism and historicism. His argument for supporting this historical position is fascinating. The contention amounts to the argumentation that such churches have always existed because such churches have always had to exist. Morphologically, there is nothing new about such conceptualization. Such reasoning has affinity to Thomistic scholasticism, natural law theory, and Scottish Realism (see chapter 2). To put the Landmarkist point another way: If you cannot believe that God has always seen to it that true churches carry out his message and ministry, and that they have been kept alive providentially, what can you believe? This datum is true because it must be true. Commencing with a premise, in due course you infer a necessary conclusion. Baptist successionism is true because it must be. By merely calling attention to the succession, Graves and his colleagues had restored validity. (Readers may realize that this reasoning is more Roman Catholic than Baptist, indeed is not Baptist theology at all.)

This is another instance in which similarities in thinking appeared under various names and in several contexts in nineteenth-century America. This Landmark Baptist tradition, along with Charleston and Sandy Creek, has continued to attract followers and contribute to the stream. In fact, two sizable Landmark fellowships arose in 1905 and 1950, respectively, the American Baptist Association and the Baptist Missionary Association of America. But these actual organizations built upon convictions and alliances that had been in process for a half century.

Separate Baptists and Primitive Baptists emerged from something that already existed and were protest movements, whether one judges them in a positive or negative light. But the circumstances of their formation are quite different from those enveloping Landmark origins. Separates and Primitives arose before there was a developed, modern, organized Baptist system of thought and cooperative life. The Separates— originally more of them were Congregationalists than Baptist (or Presbyterians)—were protesting against lifeless, formal religion that had more to do with custom and head than with heart and emotions. Their action is better captured as adding to what already existed in hopes of infusing it with new vigor than as rejecting and leaving. The Primitive Baptists resisted a tide they saw gaining strength; they set themselves aside and apart in the interest of maintaining purity. In neither case was there a systematically ordered and fully organized body from which to sever themselves. And neither desired to found a new denomination.

By contrast, the Landmark Baptists isolated heresy, railed against it, and militantly withdrew in order to preserve the Baptist message, indeed fundamental Baptist—a virtual synonym for Christian—integrity. By the 1850s there was an organization, an established, recognized body, to attack and leave.

As a matter of fact, the very fact of an organization had a great deal to do with the Landmarkists' stridency and high dudgeon over the obligation to secede. For Graves and his brothers, "boardism" was a noxious departure from true Baptistism. Setting up agencies and boards in a headquarters somewhere bespoke a denial of local church authority. This was serious because "local church" was a redundancy. The local church is what there is and all there is. The truth, and the whole truth, according to God's revelation, is that the church is universal and visible. The minute a real church participates in something higher or larger than itself, it has denied its character and, what is worse, sold its soul. A companion deviation was the whole notion of "delegates." That is to say, no church can delegate its powers to delegates. When congregations meet to have fellowship, they may send messengers, but such people are properly "messengers to represent its views and wishes" and no more.

This conflict, long simmering, reached a boiling point by 1898 or so. Schism was soon to occur. But so radical a departure had not been predictable even a few years earlier. As historian James E. Tull has written, the Landmark leaders "had associated ecclesiological heterodoxy with theological heterodoxy in their attack upon other denominations. It was a long time, however, before this association was applied to the Southern Baptist fellowship itself."[13] Several conditions account for this long period of relative peace with the large convention itself. An especially fascinating one is the reluctance to attribute this heresy to the true church(es) (Baptist, of course), which in turn might invite the sundering of the pure succession. A situation in which Baptists disowned Baptists would be the ultimate in culpatory conduct.

But things went too far; the Southern Baptist Convention embraced boardism more and more, and revealed no discernible bad conscience on the issue. Accordingly, various small schisms occurred, resulting with the passage of time in the formation of the American Baptist Association (between 1895 and 1905) and the Baptist Missionary Association of America (between 1902, when that body began, and 1950, when it took its present name). When the propensity for being correct at nearly any cost is so great, rumblings and earthquakes are apt to be continued, and they have been so in the Landmark Baptist case. Texas and Arkansas have always been the strongholds of Landmark following, but their influence has invaded Southern Baptist life in the border areas, the mid-South, the Deep South, and the Southwest. The drama of Landmark activity is captured by the fact the principal opponents of the early schismatic tremors, well-known Southern Baptists J. B. Cranfill, B. H. Carroll, J. M. Carroll, and J. B. Gambrell, were all themselves theological Landmarkists.

Landmark beginnings were focused in the mid-South, west Tennessee, southern Kentucky, and eastern Arkansas especially, which was also an early Churches of Christ hotbed—the southern "Christians." The ranks of both groups enlarged, and their weapons were sharpened as they contended for the souls of the growing—and not yet much churched—population. Historians Richard Hughes and Leonard Allen put their fingers right on the religious mood of that time and place. These resolute Restorationists argued with invective and passion. The rival bodies, Baptists and Churches of Christ especially, were locked in competition in a "great free market of souls." Their behavior was as American as apple pie.[14]

DIVERSITY ALSO HAS a racial hue. Few episodes in Baptist life, or in the history of the American South, are more significant than the emergence of independent black churches in the months and years following the close of the Civil War when legal emancipation took effect. Everyone treating this topic is startled by the alacrity of church formation. Although no independent black denominations were organized for a time (the Colored [now Christian] Methodist Episcopal Church appeared in 1870 and the National Baptist Convention in 1895, with precursor entities anticipating both), all-black congregations, self-organized and self-led, sped into being. Before long, church buildings were rising. Soon thereafter local lay leadership boards, Sunday schools, and protomissions agencies appeared. Ministers, some with preaching experience in the churches of the prewar period, visible and invisible, biracial or black (all beholden to white monitoring), assumed pastorates. In the process, they were forging the first widespread profession in the African American culture of the South.[15]

Equally arresting is the nature of institutional life among southern black people during slavery and what happened to this condition following 1865. Hardly a single standard human and social institution—family, education, politics, economics, or religion—enjoyed the opportunity to develop normally during the antebellum period. It is, of course, the nature of enslavement to prevent the enslaved from taking command of their own destiny. Family fared somewhat normally in a number of instances. Education, once encouraged, had been legally shut down by the mid-1840s after every state took steps to prohibit strides toward literacy. Politics and economics—does a word need to be spoken on these topics? And the ramifications of almost total inexperience with public life, and with the creation and management of wealth, became painfully clear during and after Reconstruction. The gasp of fresh air inhaled from voting and working gainfully was heady for a few years. But suffocation soon set in. Voting rights were rescinded and tenant farming came close to being the sole occupation of choice, therefore not really much of a choice. (The more I know about the huge void in slaves' and the freed people's political and economic experience, the closer I come to a degree of appreciation for the philosophy of uplift that dominated the thinking of black leadership as well as white.)

The freed men and women who knew much about personal religious experience also knew something about church life. Here they possessed a measure of competence. This was due in part to its being the one area where they were not interactive with or dependent upon their white neighbors. Recognition of this condition illuminates the tiny extent to which things had changed since slavery. The arenas of daily life in which there was no interaction with or dependence upon white people for determining the affairs of black people were extremely limited. The church and a few voluntary associations nearly exhausted the list. Yet as religion scholars C. Eric Lincoln and Lawrence H. Mamiya note, post-Emancipation blacks did establish mutual aid societies, fraternal lodges (that had auxiliaries for women), insurance companies, banks, and benevolent and burial associations. They conclude that the churches were the spawning waters for all those enterprises.[16]

Thus church buildings, church fellowship, and church organizations played a uniquely forceful part in the life of the black community in the late century. One other dimension informed church life centrally: the theology of the black churches. The first impression gained by a white visitor to such a service might have been that while the style was distinctly African American, the substance of hymn, prayer, and sermon was characteristically southern evangelical. In other words, the underlying message would be that of human sinfulness and divine forgiveness, the two opposing actions merging in a person's conversion experience.

This turns out to be not entirely accurate. Some subtle shifting had been taking place among black Christians as they developed an indigenous theology. The message of sin, guilt, grace, forgiveness, conversion, and righteous living remained fundamental. But emphases changed as the people's context was changing. From this period on, the black church was not to ask first, who belongs–who does not, who is saved–who is not, as the controlling issue of preaching and teaching. Efforts to convert continued, as did joy resulting from a manifest conversion. But what began to impel black worship and service to God was more collective than individual. The composition of the black church became less those who had been converted and were members than the whole people, the black community at large, whether local at large, or general and inclusive. One's identity was first and foremost black, Negro, African American. Such a perspective did not nullify churchmanship, of course, nor did it eradicate concern for fellow black people whose conduct of life made it clear that they were not yet under the direction of God's spirit. Just the same, the real "other" was white people, not disobedient black people.

Moreover, biblical perspectives changed somewhat. The Old Testament scriptures about the people of God attained new depths of meaning. Worshipers heard more and more about the Israelites' slavery in Egypt, the deliverance by God through the parted waters, wanderings in the wilderness, and glimpses of the Promised Land. Here in the Scriptures of ancient Israel, southern black people claimed identification, a powerful dynamic, at the deepest levels. They saw themselves as a new people under God, not precisely a new Israel, of course. Their lot had been betrayal, exploitation, and—they praised the Lord—deliverance, their good fortune a new journey with hope toward freedom. This good news is captured beautifully in Joseph Washington's words: "Black Folk Religion [is the] quest of black folk for freedom, justice, dignity, and equality of opportunity in this world because they knew it to be realized in the world to come." Hope here is predicated on the way things are in God's heaven, not a means to it. They had come upon a distinctive and right-headed theological insight.[17]

Clearly, sacred and secular categories were blended into one, their God caring for the mundane and the eternal. The destiny of a particular racial group with a unique historical heritage in the United States of America acquired independent significance, one that equalled the earthly-heavenly pilgrimage of one of God's creatures toward salvation. The former did not, by any means, supplant the latter. The complex presence of two distinct but interlacing concerns and the power of two images of the Lord's concern was making everything different in the African American understanding. The theology of the black churches was Christian, Protestant, and evangelical—no mistaking that—but it was also African American.

All available evidence discloses that the classic cosmic and religious philosophy of African traditional religions was monistic: the sacred and the secular are indivisible because reality is a single whole. Their thinking was not dualistic; they denied that the sacred realm is one entity, the secular another. Perhaps we will never know how much of that cosmology persisted in African American sensibilities after the Middle Passage and the lapsing of two centuries. Minimally, we can note that by post-Emancipation times Afro-Christianity had adopted a functional monism. God was not the spirits of the ancestors or tribal deities; he was the Jehovah of Israel, the Father God of Jesus, and the Lord of the apostles. But all fused into one, the sacred and the secular, to use concepts fashioned in the Euro-American heritage.

What we know of the sermons and theology of black preachers between 1865 and 1900 (and later) reveals how firmly they held to this functional monism. There was no "gospel" and "social gospel," no this-is-vertical responsibility and that-is-horizontal responsibility. Where such thinking appears, it reflects European origins. The point of this was captured well by the Rev. Lucius Holsey, a Georgia Methodist former slave who was a founding leader of the Colored Methodist Episcopal Church. His sermons hold up the fatherhood of God and the brotherhood of man. Never mind that the preacher selected for inclusion here is Methodist, rather than Baptist; the message of all the black churches was remarkably similar. Enough sermons are extant from black Baptist and black Methodist churches to indicate that, to date anyway, more and better-developed Methodist sermons exist than Baptist ones, but the message was much the same.[18]

Holsey's sermons (along with many others) reveal that the revivalistic tradition of southern Protestantism was familiar territory for black ministers. Their theology was standard evangelical fare, namely sin and salvation, the call to righteousness, Bible, and church. At the foundation was a full-fledged commitment to supernatural Christianity. No problem loomed here with belief in miracles, answer to prayer, life after death, and the inspiration of Scripture. When inquiring into any religious community's beliefs, the seeker must sedulously attend to the entire span of its teachings, avoiding singling out one or two or even a few. The point is to penetrate the system, the network, the coordination of the list of doctrines. They must be seen as some kind of whole, not merely seriatim. It follows that to say no more than that standard evangelical fare was basic to the preaching of the post-Emancipation black churches would be misleading. We must look further.

The other rich complex of teachings had to do with the brotherhood of man. Just as important, the messages about God and about humanity were coordinated, making up a dynamic whole. Even dialectics as a trope fails to do justice to the systemic character of this theological thinking. These black Christians did more than array heavenly and earthly teachings side by side. They coordinated them in such a way that neither was isolated, neither one deemed more basic than the other. The presence of each affected, limited, enlarged, modified the other. The whole and the sum of the parts were not identical. Thus, black church theology created its own character and texture, diverging from white church theology. While it departed scarcely an inch from the tradition of the region, still it invented a new compound. *Invented* is hardly an excessive word here, since comparison between this black church theology and the emerging Social Gospel theology of northern white church theology does not clarify or enhance the analysis very much. The sovereignty, graciousness, and fatherhood of God were not in question. In the words of the Rev. E. W. D. Isaacs, "the brotherhood of man is as much an integral part of Christianity as the fatherhood of God. Whoever denies either is an infidel." Working for racial justice, caring for those in need, and comprehensively embodying biblical injunctions about loving one's neighbor were basic, simply basic.

This coordination of two central Bible themes—the first two commandments, about loving God and loving the neighbor—stands, in my judgment, as one of the epochal theological achievements in American Christian history. Neither northern liberal Social Gospel nor southern revivalistic evangelicalism, the black church theology crafted in the late nineteenth century was sui generis. A century later we enjoy a vantage from which to view its integrity and forcefulness.

The crucible of a new freedom that was more official than effectual helped produce this black church theology. But, like everything else, it had some rootage. Margaret W. Creel's findings from research among the Gullahs of the South Carolina coastal islands during the antebellum period unearth some of those roots. By the 1830s, an indigenous theology was appearing. True to form, blacks and whites in the churches devoted much energy to converting and instructing the slaves in the Christian faith. But once converted and instructed, the slaves fashioned their own interpretation of the message. God was personified as Jesus; more Jesus-talk than God-talk flowed from their musical lips. The services were filled with the spirit of a fervent zest for living, consistent with their keen identification with Jesus' suffering, crucifixion, and resurrection. Other features Creel turned up were related. Everywhere a desire for liberty was enunciated. "Shouts," a routine part of services, were triumphant rather than doleful or tragic. Communal fulfillment stood out as a powerful element in the attraction of the church to the Gullah slaves. All these features rested on a new theology that held up the Eternal One as driven by love and mercy, not wrath and judgment. The Gullah theology, thus, proved to be rudimentary toward the cultivation of an innovative theology during the early decades of black church independence.[19]

BAPTIST DIVERSITY RANGED from Southern Baptist Convention variety, to antimission Baptists, to black Baptist forms. But the list goes on. Nowhere is the distance greater than between black theology and church life, on the one hand, and Baptist Fundamentalism, found almost exclusively in the white community, on the other. That Fundamentalist subcommunity is the final Baptist group to be considered here, with some traits of African American Baptist life serving as the transition. The Christianity of the black church bespeaks heart religion. It is inherently communal. It coordinates; it is not given to drawing up a list of essential doctrines, ranked by priority. That is to say, its theology has about it systematic coordination. This stands in sharp contrast to Fundamentalism.

Fundamentalists, most of them Baptist, are relative newcomers to the South. Notwithstanding the popular tendency to call the region Fundamentalist territory, both the title and the cohort appeared on the American scene early in the twentieth

century. A response, generally a reaction, to modern developments in thought, the social sciences, biblical study, and biology, the people and movement correctly so called knew where
they stood and dug in intransigently. *Modern* is a key word here
because it was modernization that they opposed so bitterly,
particularly in areas of philosophical and scientific thought.
They branded all such destructive forces "modernism." Darwinian theories of biology and higher criticism of the Bible became singularly obnoxious to Fundamentalists.

It is hardly surprising that these soldiers of the Lord's truth
were conscripted in the North earlier and in much larger
numbers than in the South. The fiercest battles were fought
in the 1920s and in northern Baptist and northern Presbyterian circles. In the colleges, universities, and seminaries of
the Northeast and Midwest, some of them denomination-
supported, the new heresies had already been promulgated for
a couple of generations. Enough time had elapsed for ministerial training to reflect this new thought, for that to filter to the
congregations, and for impious philosophies to infiltrate the
public schools and even the public. Add to these departures
from time-honored truths and modes of thinking a radically
reconfigured society, and you have a powder keg. All around
were foreigners, newly enlarged cities, new social diseases,
Catholics, and Jews. A growing number of people were asking
not only what can you trust but also whom can you even
know and know well enough to rely on. Intellectual and social
dislocation were wreaking havoc.

This familiar history of the northern states, explains much
about the South. Those demographic and social conditions
were largely absent from the South, even piecemeal, and certainly had not intruded with enough force to disrupt southern
folkways and public policy. But the public schools were feeling
the burden of the new biology; people in many other places
than Rhea County, Tennessee, the site of the Scopes trial, were
sickened and angered by the implicit denial of the veracity of
the Bible that was creeping into classrooms and laboratories.

In response, one southern state after another passed antievolution laws and a hundred skirmishes broke out in denominational conventions, college trustees meetings, and sundry local public meetings. The imagined demonic legions were not as pervasive or as influential as the pure-in-head feared, either on the desecration of the Genesis creation narrative or on the scholarly study of the Bible. The occasional heretic had been popping up since the 1880s, but all such menaces were shunted aside or silenced. Nothing smacking of a genuinely liberal or radical program was infesting seminary or college or Sunday school classrooms, not even with stealth. But fear and concern persisted, contributing heavily to the rise of a Fundamentalist sector. Among Baptists this company, rather small in numbers of churches, ministers, and lay followers, organized in the 1930s and soon (1938) was calling itself the World Fundamentalist Baptist Missionary Fellowship. They promoted their work by means of new Bible institutes and independent colleges, by composing and printing their own teaching materials and periodicals, and by setting up alternative summer camps for young people.

By and large, they did not join interdenominational fellowships or pursue an adamantly separatist course. They retained membership in the Southern Baptist Convention, without, however, mustering great enthusiasm for and a primary loyalty to that now huge, also heavily organized, denomination. In fact, what mostly drove these Fundamentalist Baptists of the South was their opposition to "unscriptural institutionalism," as one leader put it. All the campaigns and programs were many too many—and man-made besides. Their other enemy was "unionism," that is, any flirtation with cooperative Christianity, or ecumenism, which they just knew would result in compromising doctrine and yoking true believers with unbelievers.

The most significant aspect of this 1930s to 1950s southern Fundamentalist movement among white Baptists is that a Fundamentalist subculture did not result, in the interpretation of historian William Glass, either by intention or as an unexpected by-product. Regional identification and denominational loyalty persisted. In other words, the Southern Baptist Convention remained the preferred company of choice to the overwhelming proportion of the people. It was conservative without being Fundamentalist, and it was both in the region geographically and of it culturally.[20]

A forthcoming study by Mark T. Dalhouse on Bob Jones University and its network of influence will tell the story of an extremist, separatist variety of Fundamentalism present in the South from the university's founding in 1926 down to 1990. I note only that the school's student body is largely from northeastern and midwestern states, the lone exception being South Carolina, in which the school has been located since 1947 and from which it has not drawn heavily until quite recent years. Similarly most of its graduates who serve as pastors carry out their callings in northern areas. The university, a sort of quasi-denomination in itself, has made inroads into the South, especially through Christian schools. But its presence has not weakened the older regional denominations; nor has it succeeded in establishing independent Fundamentalism as a competitive rival. In most communities its brand of conservative Protestantism continues to be viewed as somewhat alien, even outlandish.[21]

Before turning to the "Christians," I review a few dominant facts concerning the Baptists:

They were in the region before 1700.
At least four major subtraditions constitute the stream that flows in the largest body, the Southern Baptist Convention.
New, dissenting bands of Baptists appeared in the nineteenth century.
Black Baptist membership and organizations expanded exponentially after the Civil War.
Fundamentalism has been comparatively weak in a society anchored by a conservative Baptist body and in which modern

currents of thought that demanded resistance came slowly and as recently as the 1940s had failed to capture the regional mentality. (Conditions have altered greatly since 1980.)

The Baptist drama, larger than life though it is, shares the southern stage with others that also have had colorful careers in a region that has been located "south of God" on some wag's great cosmic map.

CHAPTER 2

The "Christians"

ONE OF THE BOLDEST MOVES in American religious history was the decision of some Protestants during the early years of the Republic to call themselves "Christians," that is, to use that as the title for their group. Were they not that before they began referring to themselves by that designation? What about all the others who intended to stand in the religious tradition of Christianity and thought their kinsmen had been doing so for much longer than the newly self-named; were they not Christians?

The most stunning aspect of their boldness is the ease, the straightforwardness, the self-assurance involved in their calling themselves "Christians." One may fault them for naïveté or even suggest a bit of arrogance, but what prompted this development was a kind of American religious vacuum. Other denominations were all around, to be sure, but no one or two were dominant. Perhaps "vacuum" is a reductionist explanation, but the allure of seizing an opportunity is not. The time had come to set things right, in actuality to replace flawed forms with the genuine article. They were being granted a Kairotic moment in the history of the ages. They would be simply "Christian." "Back to the Bible" later became a Fundamentalist cliché. For the devout of the period 1790 to 1820, that phrase was no cliché, hardly even a rallying cry; instead it was a wide-open possibility that begged for realization.

Which bodies called themselves simply "Christians"? The earliest is the Republican Methodist Church, founded in 1793 in Virginia and North Carolina. Its most forceful leader was James O'Kelly, a Methodist minister who had never cared for the episcopacy. In 1794, the group abandoned the name Republican—itself significant since that word was electric then—in favor of the Christian Church. That title held fast until 1820, when they became the Christian Connection. In 1856, these Protestants, still strongest in Virginia and North Carolina, chose Southern Christian Conference, a designation that pulled their punch a little. By 1929, when they merged with the Congregational Church, which was descended directly from the colonial New England establishment, they had grown to 112,795 members and founded mission agencies, children's homes, and schools, most prominently Elon College—whose sports nickname remains "the fighting Christians." Ecumenism being a testament in its birthright, this body merged again in 1958 to become the United Church of Christ.[1]

To provide some insight into how these groups came to be, I examine a movement in New England that pulsed with similar concerns and lightly touched the South with its influence. Abner Jones and Elias Smith in the 1780s were hearing a divine call to reform, really re-form, the church.

No study of religious movements in the South can pretend the isolation of this one region from the rest of the national society, a condition that has been true throughout its history. One of the influences on these earliest southern "Christians" was indeed that New England stream—no surprise, since the principal direction of cultural currents in the early nineteenth century was from north(east) to south(east). In Vermont in the 1780s, a similar spirit had broken out: followers of Christ wanting only to be called Christians. They were led by Smith and Jones, Baptists restive with the imperfect state of things in that always division-prone communion.[2]

Although these two stalwarts and their fellow dissenting Baptists rarely met with the new southern Christians, these north-

ern and southern companies established warm fraternal relations by correspondence. In addition, Smith and Jones published a journal, *Herald of Gospel Liberty*, widely circulated and
read. Often greetings were exchanged. One letter sent north by
a southern Christian seems to capture the theological strictures
they all shared: there must be "no episcopacy or Calvinism
among them."[3]

As time passed, the New Englanders seemed more concerned
to forge some kind of formal unity than the southerners, thus
only informal, fraternal relations were maintained between
them. General conferences of the two groups met occasionally
until 1834 and regularly thereafter. The slavery issue managed
to divide this body, like nearly all others, but the forty-eight-
year breach was healed in 1894. Throughout, the membership
was predominantly southern.

In 1808, Jones made his way to Virginia and joined heart and
energy with O'Kelly. This Christian impetus, thus, originated
more as a function of the times than of a place. But its flowering
could take place better in an uncluttered environment. New
England was already old, and in the throes of quite a lot of religious momentum, indeed denominational patterning. New
Englanders moving to other places, including nearby upstate
New York, implanted in those places views they had been un-
able to register in the soil of the older home environment. As for
the Smith and Jones vibrations, they had seen the light of day
earlier but their fine vision took form in the South only. Smith's
convictions included vigorously acclaiming the "free individual," all being born "free, equal, and endowed." Fairly shouting
his patriotism, he heralded the reign of Christ through the
marvelous new American government. Churches too should
exemplify such freedom, permitting no molesting of a congregation's integrity by "intercongregational organization."[4]

The other principal strand of Christians is the Stone-Campbell movement, the indigenous American company of Restorationists. This significant denomination, almost the supine
embodiment of nineteenth-century American perceptions and

concerns, had its origins in two locales: first, a medley of southern Virginia, central North Carolina, and central Kentucky in the early career of Barton W. Stone between 1792 and 1804; second, the (West) Virginia panhandle and adjacent communities in western Pennsylvania and eastern Ohio. In the just-maturing society of the young West between 1806 and the 1820s, effective leadership from the Campbells—father, Thomas, and son, Alexander—both recently of Ulster, brought the Disciples of Christ into existence.

The Stone story applies to the South with particular intensity, although Barton himself moved to Illinois in 1834 partly because of his aversion to slavery. His theology attained a wide acceptance. The Campbell branch made some primary and much secondary impact on southern church life. Interaction is seen clearly in central Kentucky where before 1823 the Christian churches were Stoneite but became Campbellite. The Restoration Movement (Stone-Campbell) was not neatly regional. Just the same, regional histories and social forces attracted and repelled, rendering particular perspectives more or less acceptable. The case of the Restoration Movement remains unusually dramatic, both for having the power to overlap regional boundaries and for staking out true differentiae with such force that the sibling movements have often scarcely recognized each other.[5]

In 1832, the Stoneites and the Campbellites came together, a kind of uniting that reached official separation in the listings of the 1906 Census of Religious Bodies. That public accounting only formalized what effectively had been true for more than a half century. Truth to tell, the 1906 document's decision had as much to do with the Disciples of Christ retaining that naming as with the Churches of Christ being officially accorded that title. Both namings had long had currency. From the era of the uniting of 1832, Campbell had preferred "Disciples of Christ" and Stone "the Christian Church," although "Churches of Christ" was often the local name of choice—and, after all, name choices were local not denominational. The two major sectors of the Christian population had had less to do with each other, in no small part because of theological differences, with sectionalism only one of two major contributing factors.

The Churches of Christ were to undergo a significant shift— "from sect to denomination" is the usual way to describe such change—in the twentieth century, especially from World War I forward.[6] But from the 1840s through the 1870s, this fellowship was emphatically countercultural. It refused to take its cues, even the assumption of social responsibility, from the surrounding culture and set itself against the "progressive" Campbell wing of the movement. The basis for such radical action was its theory, derived from Stone's teaching. Its stance was apocalyptic, here referring only lightly to the Second Coming or the end of the present historical order. Rather, the heart of its apocalypticism lay in teaching transcendent values, those of God and his Kingdom, which are of another order entirely from those of any human beings or institutions, including the state and society, and of course the institutional church.

The Christian Church, or Disciples of Christ, eventually forsook their anti-institutional stance and became a major ecumenical organization. In the 1820s and 1830s Alexander Campbell had opposed institutionalizing the church, regarding societies as unbiblical. While not an exclusivist, he was intent on a purity he associated with keeping clear of human inventions and all man-made institutions. That perspective began to blur in the late 1840s and reached an entirely new phase in 1849, when the American Christian Missionary Society (ACMS) was organized. *Organized,* so innocuous a word in our vocabulary, was a revolutionary occurrence in that setting. A man-made institution, a human invention to which the New Testament makes no reference, had appeared—had been organized. The ACMS was national in breadth, not confined to the Campbellian heartland north of the Mason-Dixon line. This new departure fed the divergence that had already begun between the less-worldly, mostly southern Christians and the more progressive, largely northern Restorationists.

Much later, in 1927, the northern Disciples company was to be further fractured. In the eyes of this new breakaway fellowship, so severely had those heirs of Stone and Campbell departed the heritage that a sizable company of protesters concluded they could no longer call the deviators kinsmen. Accordingly they formed the "independent Christian churches," the third major branch of the tradition. That branch came later, in 1971, to refer to themselves as Christian Churches and Churches of Christ. While present in the South, notably in Kentucky and east Tennessee, this fellowship is strongest in new areas, such as the Pacific Northwest and the stronghold areas of the Disciples, from Ohio west across the Midwest.

Confusing as the nomenclature may be to observers, one item is perfectly clear. All the title choices were deliberate: Christian, Churches of Christ, Disciples of Christ, and independent. Those trace out a picture. Nothing institutional or otherwise man-made was acceptable to them. They meant to be "Christians only." Fairly often, the people of this heritage have "name called" toward other denominational Christian people. Especially in the early decades, Baptist, Methodist, Presbyterian, Lutheran, and all the other namings were regarded by "Christians" as human fabrications, not biblical references or titles.

This degree of denominational self-consciousness was also cropping up elsewhere within southern church life, though in a different context. At an 1844 meeting of the Kehukee Primitive Baptist Association in eastern North Carolina, the messengers approved a resolution condemning what they called a "new thing," namely Baptists organizing missionary societies. In fact they reviled such Baptists as being no better than "Methodists, Presbyterians, Episcopalians, Quakers, Campbellites, or Catholics."[7] Primitive Baptists were hearing about the heretical behavior of other so-called Christians, including Campbellites (that is, Disciples of Christ) who were selling out to newfangled ideas from modernizing culture. Whether these rather provincial Primitive Baptists knew about the Stoneites—

mostly far to their west in Tennessee—is undocumented. Most likely that band of Baptists and the Stoneites would have found little cause for nestling in common support of church causes. But on the subject of modernization, they were as one.

Even this quick sketch of Protestant name-groups that were calling themselves simply "Christians" in the nineteenth-century South reveals quite a diversity. But the point is not driven home adequately without the realization of how much dissenting existed within the Stone-Campbell movement. How did this nondenomination retain the semblance of fellowship it did? Thirty years ago historian David Edwin Harrell spoke of the "significant and almost endless diversity within the church [the Disciples]."[8] So much for the assurance that awareness of the unity of Christ's body would knit its members; so much also for the anticipated results of the faithful's acknowledgment that the New Testament clearly laid out belief and practice. Still, these Christians kept on affirming freedom as a touchstone of faith. Positive commitment to freedom *from*— in this case creeds, clerics, and institutions—seems always to bring with it a kind of indefensible freedom *for*—choosing one emphasis over another, outdoing the others in your zeal for purity and authenticity.

I return now to the earliest southern Christians, recalling that the Republican Methodist Church came into being in 1793. The chief instigator was James O'Kelly, a Methodist Episcopal Church minister, Virginia-born of Scots-Irish extraction. (It is possible that he was born in Ireland.) He never had liked the episcopacy, an opinion he had not hesitated to voice. However, stating O'Kelly's views thusly is to understate the vigor and persistence of his dissent. Almost from the start, that is, his conversion in the mid-1770s and becoming a lay preacher in Methodist societies soon after, he was a "troublemaker." Noting three instances makes the point. First, he was captured by Tories during the American Revolution but refused to swear allegiance to the king. Thereafter he served in the colonial army. Second, he and a group of lay preachers of Virginia and North Carolina ordained themselves and then others, convinced that a calling to preach carried with it a calling to sacramental administration. They were soon to be properly ordained in the new (1784) Methodist Episcopal Church. Third, O'Kelly challenged Francis Asbury's assumption of rights as a bishop from the beginning; similarly he challenged a particular superintendent's legitimacy and authority. "Troublemaker" is an apt term for him—emphatically so in the eyes of the new Methodist organization.[9]

With the passing of the years, matters between O'Kelly and the Methodist Episcopal Church did not improve, as O'Kelly devoutly envisioned the way God's church should constitute itself. The rift steadily widened. On several issues and decisions he opposed Asbury who brooked dissent testily. Especially did O'Kelly stand up against "invasion of the civil and religious liberties of the people." Seeing no hope for a relaxation of centralized polity, he and a small band of confreres withdrew, latching on to "republican," then a magical term, as a suitable symbol of their convictions. This did not erupt without officialdom's efforts to placate the O'Kellyites. Compromises were offered, especially as conciliatory gestures. But nothing silenced these rebellious church people. The "desire for more democracy in the church" impelled their actions. A breach developed at the 1792 General Conference of the Methodist Episcopal Church. When the "evils of episcopal government" were not addressed and repented of, the dissenting band had no choice but to separate. Nothing changed when they began to call themselves the Christian Church a few months later. But already they had attracted quite a following. In the first year, more than one thousand Methodists became "Christians." The ranks included ministers of note, especially Rice Haggard who was to serve as a link with the Christian movement developing west of the Appalachian mountains under the principal early impetus of Barton Stone's powerful leadership in Kentucky, Ohio, and Tennessee. Haggard was in fact responsible for Stone and his followers accepting the name "Christian." The idea was not one he generated west of the mountains; far from it. At the 1794 gathering in Surry County, Virginia, where the Republican Methodists became Christians, Haggard had made the difference. Holding up a New Testament, he declaimed: "by it we are told that the disciples were called Christians and I move that henceforth and forever the followers of Christ be known as Christians simply." A subtle point that Haggard was making needs underscoring here: "Christian" is not a denominational label, it is "our name," so to speak.[10]

One truly major minister, William McKendree, joined the O'Kelly-led company for a time. But after discovering for himself that Bishop Francis Asbury was more and less than a power broker (even that his episcopal credentials were questionable) and withal an effective man of God, McKendree returned to the church's fold and himself became its foremost episcopal officer on the early western frontier in the South.

Lacking in effective leadership this new company was not, nor in well-wrought and vigorously held positions. In sentiments that anticipated and paralleled the Stone and Campbell contentions, they "renounced all human institutions in the church as a form of 'popery' not fit for the discipline of human souls." One basis for this declaration was their self-description as "free citizens in the land of Columbia."[11]

What these true-blue Americans wanted was, first, a democratic polity; but they also believed in church unity. They surely are among the earliest ecumenists, although they were not keen on formal unification. The unity of all Christians seemed to them irrefutably appropriate; more than that, obligatory. When a community's normative test is so plain, they reasoned, how can a discerning people stumble into uncertainties of human creation—uncertainties that are both artificial and divisive? Their keynote was straightforward: we are called to be the church "without the shackles of written credo or dictatorial hierarchy."[12]

Here is a stunning instance of the democratarian spirit taking root in the populace: freedom. In this case, freedom *from* institutional control and *for* popular lay participation and leadership. It is worth underscoring that the ecumenical spirit persisted, leading to a uniting of like-minded bodies in the southern region in 1847, long before the mergers of 1929 and 1958. As for the polity reform that engineered the mergers, that vision continued and, with modifications, remains the way in which these southern Christian churches govern themselves. They do this today as members of the United Church of Christ that was organized in 1958. The Southern Christian Conference and, later, the Congregational Christian Churches were themselves an amalgam of several groups. The principal allies in the new merger were the old New England Puritan body of Congregationalists, and the Evangelical and Reformed Church, a kind of German American Methodism that had been present in some force among Virginians and Carolinians of German descent since the 1750s.

While the more prominent company of Christians in the nineteenth-century South were those committed to Restorationism in the heritage of Barton W. Stone and Alexander Campbell, the earlier Christians should not be taken too lightly. The O'Kelly movement was unmistakably an indigenous southern formation. Its leaders and members were in and of the South. Its legacy has been primarily regional. Also its political rootage attaches a singular attribute to it. There can be no doubt that the winds and waves of O'Kelly's lifetime (1735–1826) were democratic, or perhaps I should say republican. That he aspired to pure New Testament teaching on church governance is clear. But the political currents of the time contributed mightily to his thinking. The concerns of Stone and Campbell were much more focused on ecclesiology. They were less interested in American democracy than in the "democratization of Christianity in America." They would not have wanted to attribute much, if any at all, of their views of the church's constitution to political influence. They were, instead, calling the church to acknowledge its constitution, the Bible, which "happened to" prohibit government "from the top-down."

Stone was born in Maryland in 1772, soon moved with his family to southside Virginia, experienced conversion while a student at David Caldwell's Presbyterian academy in Guilford County, North Carolina, then was borne out to central Kentucky on the flood tide of enthusiastic evangelicalism in 1798. As a Presbyterian pastor, he sparked the Cane Ridge revival of 1801 that burst local boundaries in the Great Revival of that near-west frontier for nearly a decade. Perhaps surprisingly, then, Stone's lasting contributions had something to do with the life of the mind, as well as with the expressions of the spirit. Authenticity was in the air. What the Bible said about the organization of congregational life and what Christians properly believe took a premier place on the churches' agendas. Any conclusions drawn must be totally in line with the Scriptures—by which they really meant the New Testament. It followed that they must restore the primitive church. Could anything be more obvious than the necessity of Restoration? Perhaps not.

For most other Protestants, however, that goal was not achievable. That was then, this is now, with many "thoses" in the interim. That is to say, much history has intervened, producing modifications, also God's breaking forth more light from his Holy Word, as the pilgrim John Robinson stated it. Repristination might be desirable in some sense, but it is not possible. All other Christian bodies have wanted either to link the new with the original or recover the heart and soul of the normative for Christian belief and practice. Restoring, restituting, repristinating was another matter.

Stone and his colleagues had greater faith. They went to work in 1803 to formulate a kind of creed, the Springfield Will and Testament, that directly reflected their negative assessment of Presbyterian ways. It stated their resolve to "remove all obstacles which stand in the way of [God's] work, and give him no rest till he make Jerusalem a praise in the earth." This bold ambition was not intended for these presbyters and their fellow denominationalists alone, but was a call to all Christians to employ common sense and good judgment, seeing the light and acting on it. The call was an optimistic one that looked to the future. *Millennial* is the technical description; postmillennial comes closer to precisely characterizing their view of the economy of God, although their transcendent theology was more apocalyptic than strictly millennial.[13]

The spirit of the Springfield document was viewed as a kind of companion to the Bible, although the next year (1804) they saw that the document itself was man-made and dissolved it, writing of its "Last Will and Testament." That revocation helped stake out the ground for the debate that was to lead to the Disciples' vigorous denunciation of all human institutions, anything man-made, in favor of the churches restoring the teachings of the New Testament on the issues of authority, doctrine, and church polity. Accordingly, it denounced the presbytery to which the ministers had belonged, indeed that they had created; it rejected all ecclesiastical laws; and it placed all responsibility for a church's practice in the hands of that church itself. One rallying declaration was "unity," unity of all in the Body of Christ—as restored of course. Accordingly, they pronounced a judgment on all divisions of Christ's followers, including specific denominations and the entire concept of denominationalism. These early Disciples were not another denomination, not a denomination at all. They were emphatic in this view, to the point of making undenominationalism the defining quality of their identity.

From that juncture on, especially from the 1840s forward, this family called Christians has had to wrestle with the implications of its dedication to restoration, unity, and nondenominationalism. The various consequences of holding to those views and holding them together began to fracture their common life by that momentous 1840s decade. Slightly too neatly stated, the Disciples of Christ denomination flows from the "later Alexander Campbell," who was less separatist and more institutionalist than the "early Campbell," whose convictions have been preserved by the nondenomination—the fellowship, the brotherhood, the body that is not a body and has no headquarters—called Churches of Christ.

Barton Stone also contributed very heavily to the distinction that became a differentiation that, eventually, became a division between the Disciples of Christ and the Churches of Christ. The latter, identified as the southern wing of the movement, really drew upon his theological perspective; more aptly, on his particular rendering of restorationism. This is seen more clearly after the Stone and Campbell unification of 1832 when the nuances of the unique view of each come to light. Stone and Campbell were busy writing, speaking, and preaching what their messages were—more often compatible than at variance. But by the 1840s, largely irrespective of the two founders, two legacies were forming, Stone's in the South and Campbell's in the Midwest (not exclusively, of course). When those messages left their hands, the public claimed them, different publics, opting differently, adding a dash of creativity. Two points emerge with great salience: (1) the differences between them became clearer in what the brotherhood variously adopted than it ever had in the interaction between the two reformers; (2) the power of Stone's formulation made one sectional appeal, the power of Campbell's another. (Neither branch has ever made much headway in the Middle Atlantic or the northeastern states.)

Because this is a study of the South, I pay greater specialized attention to Stone than I might have otherwise. Indeed it is only in the recent research of historian Richard T. Hughes on the Churches of Christ that the Stoneite-Campbellite differentiation has come so forcefully to light. Not surprisingly, Stone's growing up years in the very southern Pittsylvania County, Virginia, and his period of study in David Caldwell's academy seventy-five miles south in North Carolina, did a great deal to shape his outlook. Once he settled in the West he led the Cane Ridge revival and helped form, then dismantle, the Springfield Presbytery. Both types of courses were genuinely his. But his inner heart beat more to the rhythm of piety than to rationality.

Hughes has elaborated a characterization of Stone-the-reformer alongside his cofounder, Alexander Campbell. Campbell's reform was rational and cognitive, generating a concern with forms and structures. He was unmistakably a child of the Enlightenment; in that sense, a scientist and a modern man.[14] Campbell was also decidedly an optimist, truly a postmillennialist, a progressive; it is not too much to say that he was "a liberal." From the late 1830s (he died in 1866), he was increasingly making his peace with a changing society, even contributing to its shifting mentality. That this extended even to his embracing the institutionalization of the church, as in his support of the American Christian Missionary Society in 1849, dramatically seals the point. His lifelong emphasis on the twin themes of Restoration and Christian unity persisted. But his placing the former in the service of the latter took some of the steam from Restoration, rendering it less radical and him less single-minded. True to form for a modern rational man, he thought in means-ends terms; meaning, in this application, that the once ever-so-powerful Restoration theme became less radical, therefore less compelling.

The Stoneite wing of the party took over in the South. It too underwent changes, but its punch was direct, muscular, effective. Barton Stone was, in Hughes's words, a child of the First and Second Great Awakenings that erupted in the period between 1745 and 1810.[15] His fellow Presbyterians were central players in that effervescence—indeed one of them had launched the southern phase; Samuel Davies in Virginia came down from William Tennent's Log College, the school of the prophets, near Philadelphia. During his Presbyterian academy student days, Stone was converted, not merely educated.

Thus there is continuity between Stone's upbringing and education in revival territory in the East and his igniting evangelistic fires at Cane Ridge in Kentucky. The South was his home; it shaped him and it incorporated his impact. If Campbell's reform was rational and cognitive, concerned with forms and structures, Stone's was ethical; the meaning of discipleship in and of the people, the members, is what drove him.[16] He was an ecclesiastical particularist who strove to recover the true church against any denominations and the entire concept of denominationalism. That was one of his sectarian visions. The other was even more radical, his commitment to affirming the values of the Kingdom of God and rejecting the values of this world. The first rejection-affirmation put him out of step with American (and European) church developments that had come to be taken quite for granted. The second rejection-affirmation, concerning ordinary values in a democratic society, gave him, especially his later following, an odor of arrogance and irresponsibility. The first made his church a sect; the second made his movement sectarian. Its adherents were "come-outers," people who listened to a different (and offbeat) drummer.

Actually Stone's double sectarianism was of a single piece. The entire denominational structure was fallen, an arrangement contrary to the divine will and quite at variance with the New Testament's "one body of Christ" that he believed to be restorable and restoration-insistent on Christians ever since. Being Christ's disciples in Christ's own body, a brotherhood that shared (indeed is) his own by constitution and mandate offered no option to the earnest life of serious obedience.

How precisely, practically, did this vision eventuate in sectarian behavior, the embodiment of a sectarian worldview? For the majority in the nineteenth century this commitment meant abstention from political participation. Faithful disciples would not consider running for political office. Far more basically, they were not even to vote. One of the two most influential leaders of the era's southern Disciples, David Lipscomb of Tennessee, voted once, in 1860 (for John Bell); never again.[17] Dedication to no political participation, going so far as to embrace pacifism, remained a Churches of Christ distinctive until the era of World War I and following (with some 10 percent of the present-day fellowship still adhering to that come-outer position). Social conventionalists need not boggle at such behavior; a single coming to terms with the apocalyptic world-view of Barton Stone and his southern heirs, Lipscomb and Tolbert Fanning, the second influential leader, facilitates understanding. Christians should listen to the voice of God and the values he embodies and commands and not the teachings of the society and people around them. No societies are God-ordained, they inferred from the New Testament.

This version of nineteenth-century Restorationism caught on in the South. Its founding father was schooled in the region, both educationally and professionally. Beyond that, this was a movement that, from its effective inception in the 1840s and its early enlargement following the Civil War, seemed at home among poor and uneducated people. That was the South's kind of society in the rural areas of middle and west Tennessee, southern Kentucky, northern Alabama and Mississippi, Arkansas, and Texas where the movement flourished. They were of and for the poor, the working class. Their outlook did not favor fanciness or wealth or power or even the modernizing aspects of business and political life. The devastation wrought by the Civil War simply reinforced their own status and expanded the ranks of people like them. Their dedication to simple living, to basic righteousness, seemed appropriate, as well as right.

It is essential to recall that the Stone heritage was part of the larger Stone-Campbell movement. The southern Christians did not renounce Alexander the Baptizer, but began to register dis-ease with his progressive bent from the late 1830s. As early as 1844, the second of the influential leaders, Tolbert Fanning, "thought he heard the sound of compromise coming from the hills of Bethany," Campbell's home in the (West) Virginia panhandle.[18] This commentary from a full-fledged Restorationist in Tennessee stands in sharp relief to the response of Campbell's supporters and critics alike, a view well expressed by the Virginia Baptist J. B. Jeter, who welcomed the changes he was hearing of from one whose movement he harshly attacked.

The regional issue, while far from tidy, was prominent. The climax of the story appears in 1906. That year's decennial

United States Census of Religious Bodies reported membership figures of two "denominations" standing in the Restorationist movement. Hitherto the numbers were represented in a
single "Disciples of Christ" entry. Asked by the census spokesman if he thought it accurate to distinguish the two bodies,
David Lipscomb said "yes." The aggregate membership stood
at 1,142,359 in 1906. Of that total, more than 80 percent resided
in nine states: Indiana, Illinois, Iowa, Kansas, Kentucky, Missouri, Ohio, Tennessee, and Texas. The newly specific Disciples
of Christ denomination claimed almost 1 million of that number. Of that million, only 139,000 lived in the South. Removing
Virginia and North Carolina from the inventory of states netted
only 99,000 in the nine other southern states. The South was not
coterminous with Disciples country.[19]

The Churches of Christ cohort—denomination is both inaccurate and offensive—reported 157,000 members in the eleven
states of the old Confederacy. The only northern state with more
than 5,000 adherents was Indiana. Concentration was heaviest
in the Tennessee region, Arkansas, and Texas. (Kentucky, West
Virginia, Missouri, and Oklahoma, all together, were home to
only 30,000 Churches of Christ members.)

Most of the Church of Christ congregations in the South were
small, rural, and little organized, as befitted their sectarian
commitments. While the fit of the Stone perspective to southern conditions accounts partly for its co-optation of the like-
minded in the region, diverging developments in the North
contributed as well. Pressure for the split came from both sides.
Campbell's "progressive primitivism" had sunk deep roots by
1906. And what had begun rather gradually before and after
the 1840s had burgeoned as a denominational perspective took
over. The northern branch, the Disciples of Christ, grew rapidly
and organized intensely after the Civil War as the modernization process set in everywhere. Towns and cities grew, in-
dustry expanded, and the tendency to organize everything
became commonplace. Disciples' congregations often became
quite large, putting up huge buildings (many quite refined in

taste), planting Sunday schools and all sorts of benevolence societies, and even installing pipe organs. In the educational
sphere, the Disciples were founding liberal arts college, inau-
gurating the Bible Chair movement (on state-assisted cam-
puses), and setting up Disciples Divinity Houses in graduate
institutions (Chicago was the first in 1894).

Of course the Disciples' branch could have chosen other missions and courses. But circumstances would not have made
that easy for a clearly middle-class constituency in a startlingly
vibrant culture. Campbell himself had been a wealthy man.
Many in his movement were distinguished leaders in society
(including Pres. James A. Garfield). The tradition had always
fostered the life of the mind—back to Campbell's Ulster and
Scotland days. The Campbell heritage had been a major pro-
genitor of Scottish Common Sense Realism, of Baconian philosophy. The life of the mind was honored, its development
encouraged.

On the theological side, the balance in the Disciples' twin
priorities of Restoration and Christian unity was definitely shifting to the unity side. Obviously that meant inclusivity, not
exclusive withdrawal in the interest of purity. Less and less
were the Disciples living like sectarians. At root, this company
became a major voice in the liberal Protestant surge of the decades before and after the turn of this century. Compelled and
guided by external socio-cultural forces and internal theologi-
cal-ecclesiastical convictions, the Disciples' movement turned
toward the denominational structure and the inside track of the
Protestant establishment that ruled America for several decades.
Though younger and smaller than the Presbyterian, Methodist,
and Congregational communities, the Disciples became a central actor in the quest for a Christian (Protestant) America.

Things were not so down south. The Churches of Christ had
headed in a steadily, increasingly radical, countercultural direction for more than half a century by 1906. From the outside, one
might wonder at the deep division, the pell-mell pace with
which the two were parting company, since both of the themes

that bound them, Restoration and unity, had so much to do with the churches' ecclesiological doctrine. They shared at least that much. Yet the shape and dynamic that held them together soon pried them apart. The Disciples had made Restoration recessive; in fact often they simply retained its language without dedication to its enactment. The passion for unity brought down the walls of exclusivism, even of their unique identity to some degree. For the Churches of Christ, unity receded as public policy, instead becoming a staple of their separatism (that was not always an exclusivism). Unity is a biblical command, they knew, but on the Bible's terms—which other Christians were not able to see. Restoration strengthened as the watchword, this feature providing the brotherhood with a powerful sense of identity and mission. It could be argued that this came at the expense of fellowship and cooperation with other Christians. But any such argument came from the outside, for to have compromised that commitment would have added up to being faithless and disobedient, which would be unconscionable. In these ways, the sharing of two fundamental convictions relentlessly drove two branches of the same tradition far, and ever farther, apart.[20]

The Churches of Christ in the South knew what was becoming of their alienating and alienated fellow Stoneite-Campbellite kinsmen in the border and midwestern states. They summed up the course of the Disciples as fondness for fashion. Large and fine church buildings—how could you justify that behavior on New Testament grounds? Complex organizations in support of missions, education, and (worst of all) denominational activities—does a single word of the New Testament support involvements of those kinds? What about the use of instrumental music, the best-known feature of Churches of Christ practice? That had become a nonissue for the northern Campbellites, what with their splendid organs in their fine churches.[21] "Show me any defense of that practice in the pages of the New Testament," one does not have to strain to hear the southern Stoneites declare.

Both branches retained a hermeneutic of literalism, that is, a specific text-centeredness, but in the South that meant scrupulous attention to every command of the New Testament. Of course theirs was a selective "attention to every command," and of course their practices often had to do with where the Scriptures were silent. And from the perspective of the historic Protestant tradition, the Churches of Christ could see only the trees, not the forest, that is, individual verses and little of the greater (Gospel) message. The Churches of Christ aimed to defend the creed, rather than cure the sins of the age, the major misstep the northerners were taking. Their theological aversion to the Disciples was accompanied by, in fact rooted in, their disapproval of what was occurring in the northern section of American society. That had become too largely an immoral land. Alas, some of that immorality was moving southward and creeping into their godly society. Fashion and the use of "hireling pastors" in the churches could not be countenanced. Social class awareness was intensifying; the South retained the people and the conventions of the simple folk, the plain people.[22] As David Lipscomb said of interregional matters in 1891, "loose rationalistic and semi-infidel teachings are prevailing in some churches of Disciples in the northern states."[23]

Another angle on the Churches of Christ is its very name. That name refers to an unusual kind of entity, not an organization, not a simple amphictyony, not even a denomination of the Christian Church. Yet Churches of Christ has a strong heritage and evokes a degree of identity-consciousness that places it in the company of Roman Catholic, Mormon, or Southern Baptist group influence. Someone who has been reared in any of those communities of faith and culture never shakes that identity. Put crudely, they "do a number on you." Put cleanly, "I know who I am and I am grateful." Another aspect of the significance of naming is the way the name is constructed grammatically. Much ink and some blood has been spilled over whether the brotherhood is an uppercase entity, Churches, or a lowercase entity, churches. The same fastidiousness obtains with regard to the inclusion, or not, of the definite article: *the* churches of. . . . Insistence on being no denomination at all, in a world that does not know what to do with unstructured groupings, makes insiders impatient in dealing with the inflexible categories of outsiders. It may be that nowhere in American religious history is the issue of name or title so important as here, in the case of these "Christians only" who are bent on an exact restoration of the primitive church.

The Stone-Campbell movement, for all of its yearning to be different or contrarian—even countercultural—with respect to the social, political, and religious establishment participated in the currents carrying America forward during the antebellum years. In some cases, it was a creative, constructive force; in others it was an effective undertow. With respect to the southern region, these Christians served as an important conduit for piping in national ideas and opinions at a time when there was mounting resistance to alien thinking and an enlarging reliance on its own wisdom and ways.

Of course the region was no more isolated in religious perspectives than in economic and political ones. But Stone-Campbell wielded at least three strengths that made impact. One had to do partly with Campbell's vision of the special place of America in God's plan. He foresaw the millennium coming soon and believed the uniting of all Christians in the restored New Testament church would serve as a catalyst. His journal of mature and more irenic years was named the *Millennial Harbinger*. Titles of in-house organs are taken seriously in a community that has honored editors as much as others have honored bishops and that has put so much stock in the printed page. On the Stone side, at least one comparable influence appeared, Elias Smith's impact on the O'Kellyite enterprise. New Englander Smith, an ardent Jeffersonian Republican, saw the American Revolution as the beginning of the end. Through the establishment of the new nation's government one could foresee the final reign of Christ of which it was an earnest.[24] Working later, Stone himself stuck more strictly to religious subjects, going nowhere near as far as Smith had earlier and Campbell was doing currently in holding up America as an agent in the coming of God's Kingdom. But the symbiosis of America and the authentic church was a current this tradition helped deliver to the region.

A second infusion of national thinking and valuing that the Stone-Campbell movement helped provide the South was anti-slavery sentiment and an apology for it, though to a limited degree. Radicals they were not, certainly not to the extent that the spirit of Alexander Campbell prevailed. These Christians were most numerous in Tennessee and southern Kentucky; they were not residents of the portions of the South where pro-slavery feelings ran deepest and firebrand rhetoric was so common. But the system of slavery, with all its attendant ramifications, embroiled their lives. They were deeply involved in it. Their churches, like all others, had Negro members and attendees, segregated within the building. Few independent Negro congregations stood in the Christian tradition, and the number of Negro preachers was small.

Antislavery teaching and activity was one aspect of the southern Christians' outlook throughout the antebellum period, although it was more in evidence early than in the 1840s and 1850s. The Disciples had participated in the African colonization efforts early in the century. In general the brotherhood either registered some opposition to slavery or lived with something of a bad conscience on this inescapably ethical issue. Campbell himself was rather progressive on the subject, fundamentally opposing or seriously questioning slavery; and he freed the slaves who worked for him in his extensive farming and stock-raising enterprise. But this concern did not burn deep within him, and his reasons for opposing the institution were mainly expedient and rational.[25]

Campbell, by nature of a more rational temperament, came to have little time for abolitionists and their cause. This had the effect of distancing him somewhat from explicit criticisms of the "peculiar institution." In fact historian Harrell reports that after 1849 his sentiments—if not his convictions—lay with the South. He could not brook the agitation and thunderous attacks of northern abolitionists that were so audible by that time. He engaged in bitter conflicts with the northern radicals in the decade or so before the Civil War. This is inherently noteworthy, but its significance is even greater because previously he had not been party to taking sides. He wanted "no subservience to one sector of the Union" until his (mild) change of heart. Campbell did not support slavery, although his conclusion that the New Testament did not regard slaveholding as a sin affected his outlook. But on this volatile issue he was guided as much by temper, his own and that of others, as by ethical conviction. He was a moderate. He wished to be a judicious spokesman in a torn society. He preferred evolution to revolution. He could have no truck with the zealotry of agitators. He knew there was fault to be found with both sides, the radical abolitionists of the North and southerners who treated Negroes as inferior—even if some in the latter population dealt with the men and women of color rather charitably.[26] Common sense, good judgment, gradual amelioration, these terms describe the Campbellian animus. And not far beneath the surface was his inclination to segregate religious and political problems, slavery falling under the latter heading in the main. Similar views, partly owing to Campbell's impetus, were common among southern Disciples. Many preachers there persisted in their slaveholding but, by and large, they were moderates on the region's most inflammatory subject. And an occasional voice or pen was raised in support of civil disobedience, such as that of editor Isaac Errett who acknowledged a "higher law."[27]

Barton Stone's positions on slavery were different because they addressed this problem, like all earthly issues, from another perspective. He was making a statement in 1834 when he moved from Kentucky to Illinois partially driven by his opposition to slavery. But for him the heart of the matter was avoiding preoccupation with mundane matters, with the kingdom of humankind. His southern followers embraced their teacher's strong apocalyptic convictions. The Kingdom of God, the ultimate transcendent regime, can never be fully realized in history. Christians should reject the values of the world, meaning that they are apolitical, do not vote or fight, do not own slaves, and do not seek wealth and power. Nevertheless, Stone could not altogether set aside this vexing problem. Early he had supported the colonization movement. He did not shrink from saying that slavery is both immoral and unwise, that "slavery is anti-Christian." Stone's blending of interest and disinterest in the slavery issue on the part of the church is summarized by denominational scholars McAllister and Tucker this way: Following early direct activity toward alleviating the condition of black people and reaching the conclusion that human efforts could not accomplish enough, "he spent the declining years of his life in relative silence on the issue of slavery."[28] Ambivalent is not what he was, quite; nor indifferent; nor eager to be a judicious leader. His mind and heart were "set on things above," as befits a Christian apocalypticism.

Any treatment of American denominations in the nineteenth century has to raise the question of division perpetrated by sectional conflict. Did the Stone-Campbell movement divide along North and South lines over the issues of slavery and sectionalism? The apparent answer is No. In this particular, quite distinctive case, however, the facts warrant the highlighting of the question without providing an adequate answer.

Was there any unit, or entity, to divide? Organizationally there was not. Even the Disciples of Christ and the Churches of Christ, as the designations were to be called from 1906 on, did not exist. What was operative by the decades of the 1840s, 1850s, and 1860s were two emerging consensus groupings; the denomination-tending, incipiently organizing, society-friendly spiritual descendants of Alexander Campbell (in his later-life persona); and the apocalyptic-minded, sectarian soul-siblings of Barton Warren Stone. The fixed yet diverging directions of the two groups were already set. The real issue turns out to be the question, Did the sectional conflict, the war, and secession have much to do with the Stone movement becoming strongest in the South and the Campbell in the North? I submit that those political-social conditions did not. It would even be difficult to support the view that the nature of southern societal life succeeded in reinforcing a trend that had commenced a decade or two before the conflict. There was after all societal continuity in the South between its prewar and postwar years. The South as a society did not change greatly from 1850 to 1880; but its conditions surely did, hence its agenda, self-perception, and relation to the larger world.

Divergence thus preempted any likelihood of division. As the Disciples' brotherhood of the midwestern and border states pealed into step with a rationalizing modern American society, it removed itself from grassroots consideration by the agrarian southern culture. There remained sectarians in the North to be sure, and progressives in the South, as well. But the Stone "spin" on the Stone-Campbell synthesis held aloft values that were at home in the South, that could be defended there; in fact, that effectively joined the radicalism of the Restoration ideology and the ways and visions of the southerners. The issue of North-South division, therefore, illuminates the character of the Stone-Campbell movement, but turns out to be an issue they did not have to face, notwithstanding the total consumption of the eastern United States, and especially the southern states, by the raging fire of sectional conflict.

The Stone-Campbell tradition contributed three currents of thought to nineteenth-century America: the first, the role of the nation in God's plan; the second, its views on slavery. The third current is their acceptance of Common Sense philosophy, so-called Scottish Realism, a tradition of thought that informed so much popular American thinking and no small measure of sophisticated reasoning in the first half of the nineteenth century. Common Sense, using the Baconian method, underlay Alexander Campbell's intellectual formulations. Having learned about it during his single term at the University of

Glasgow (and even earlier at home in Ulster from his father, Thomas), he enveloped his biblicism in it, making it part and parcel of the Campbellian program.[29]

In the South, that program swept central Kentucky between 1820 and 1840. Also it was attracting thousands of followers in Tennessee and contiguous areas where the southern Disciples, eventually Churches of Christ, became numerous and influential. The Campbell influence only strengthened the existing Stoneite presence. Other conduits penetrated below the Mason–Dixon line too, in the small scientific and philosophical circles of the southern region. But it may be that none rivaled the Campbellian infusion for effect on the rank and file of the southern population. In the antebellum period, the cadre of elite urban pastors in several denominations, many influenced by Princeton theology, also were steeped in Common Sense and promulgated it.

Here is a stellar example of religion's power to impact a culture along lines that transcend its more limited theological or institutional concerns. The Stone-Campbell tradition had status as an alternative to the South's evangelicalism. The latter was approaching hegemonic status about the time of the Disciples movement's assault on the South. In the introduction, I classified the "Christian" grouping as one branch of that family—sort of, with reservations. Here, one is required to treat it as marginal, a highly peculiar variant on that way of thinking about Protestant meaning and comporting.

Scottish Realism is certainly not confusable with evangelical understanding. Nor for that matter does it have much in common with the classic Calvinism that stood in the near background of the South's popular theology. Scottish Realism as adapted by the Disciples clearly rejected the Calvinist concept of the sovereignty of God, and it replaced Calvin's dual emphasis on Word and Spirit, confining Spirit to the "pages of Holy Writ." It posits an innate "moral sense" in all human beings.[30] So equipped, every person has access to real knowledge of what is true and what is right. Obviously, human capacity is great; there is no need for men and women to wallow very long in the slough of ignorance concerning what is true and good. Further, it devalues the role of the learned, at any rate of those who have acquired their vast knowledge by means of other organons than Common Sense. Campbell was caustic toward doctors of divinity, ministers pretentious about their learning—the more so since they were pursuing perverse paths toward knowledge.

Two features of the southern religious landscape that resulted from the Baconian-Campbellian handiwork call for brief attention here. One is that mentality's participation in the vigorous, sometimes furious, competition that raged among the various Protestant groups recruiting members in midcentury Tennessee and Kentucky. The second is the phenomenon of lectureships. Concerning the competition, hark back to the Landmark Baptists. Although no scholarship has yet demonstrated with certainty that the Landmarkists of that same period and place were direct beneficiaries of Common Sense reasoning, I strongly suspect a connection. In the dog-eat-dog confrontations of that time, Presbyterians put down Baptists, who thundered against Campbellites, who verbally destroyed Methodists, and so on.

Such confrontations heralded an identifying ritual that the Churches of Christ have developed for a century now: the lectureships. These are annual events at such institutions as Abilene Christian, Freed-Hardeman, Harding, and several state Christian colleges. Held on a regularly scheduled basis, they draw great crowds from the brotherhood, lay people as well as preachers. Comparable to Baptist summer encampments or Methodist camp meetings, the lectureships have been "a form of religious education that . . . [serves] as a rallying center for . . . unity and orthodoxy." At times, the denominations are criticized for their false teachings, and for constituting a company of unbelievers. By and large, the lectureships serve to drive home sound doctrine. Their effect has been to "define and resolve areas of conflict, present challenges for action, and broaden the intellectual-theological consensus of Churches of Christ."[31]

The Churches of Christ lectureships can be placed alongside the revivals of southern evangelicals. Real differences exist, of course, but the functions correspond. Nineteenth-century Baptists and Methodists were converting the lost, using revivals and camp meetings to induce a keen sense of guilt before God, the grace offered by the Lord knocking at heart's door, and the glorious rapprochement of unsaved person and divine Savior resulting in the new birth toward eternal life. Many southern Disciples (though not Stone) promoted assent and right-thinking. Qualifying as anti-intellectual according to many standards, they were, nevertheless, rationalists. As such they were simply one embodiment of the authentic Stone-Campbell outlook.

To keep the record straight, Barton Stone opposed debating as a means to advancing the Christian cause. For one thing, debating leaned too heavily on rationality at the expense of the spiritual and the pious. But more important, Stone treasured freedom too much to take pleasure in bettering another Christian in a verbal discourse. He was not one to impose tests of membership or to put others on the spot. In the middle years of his leadership career, Campbell had engaged in debating, and he was quite successful at it, but Stone thought other measures worthier.[32]

Straight thinking rather than experiential conversion was the churches' central task. For these reasons, the Stone-Campbell movement in its first two generations rectified better than it recruited. It was more effective at turning the already sensitized toward the truth than it was at bringing people across the line that separates the skeptical from the believing.[33] What the movement accomplished, then, had less to do with space (the frontier) than with time (the generation following the success of the Great Awakening and the Great Revival, when vital religion was already an accessible commodity). The evangelicals had had to do their work first before the Disciples could do what they were commissioned to do. Both worked effectively.

The Stone-Campbell tradition was firmly established in the South through its successes between 1801 and 1850. Before internal migration opened the Southwest to a stable and thriving population after the Civil War, the Restorationists were strongest in central Kentucky and middle Tennessee. From Lexington northwest and northeast, the more expansive heritage of the "later Alexander Campbell" dug in to become a major religious and cultural force. From Nashville west and southwest, the stricter, more sectarian aspects of the Stone heritage were perpetuated to make that territory the Churches of Christ redoubt. Although the Restorationist memberships were somewhat localized, the tradition was alive and notable in the region, indeed was partly spawned in it. It contributed to providing the sectionalist South with some exposure to national currents of thought. Further, it seems to have widened the stream of unofficial restorationist mentality that had informed the influential Baptist subgroup called the Landmarkist. All this adds up to a major religious heritage in the South, from near-trans-Appalachia to Oklahoma and west Texas, and showing a considerable diversity.

A glimpse at the career of one southern Disciple, the Rev. James R. Lamar of Georgia, epitomizes the crosscurrents and changes characteristic of southern Disciples' life in the century's later half. Lamar began his ministry as a Campbellian in the 1850s. He adopted a strict Scottish Realism position on authority, on Scripture in particular, and on what is a suitable epistemology.[34] How do human beings know Christian truth, according to Lamar? We know by simply acknowledging that the Gospel is facts and propositions. In line with Alexander Campbell's progressivism toward learning, Lamar displayed great enthusiasm for science. As one who accredited empirical observation, he had little use for theory and abstract concepts. The title of his 1859 book, *The Organon of Scripture*, reveals a great deal. "Like science, like theology" sums up his perspective. For him, the valid categories in knowing are "certainty," "unmistakability," "self-explanatory," and "self-justifying." That is the standard strict Campbell line—which Churches of Christ have generally subscribed to, and which was to comprise part of the portfolio of the Independent Christian Churches, the third branch of the movement that came to birth in the 1920s.

For the first decades of his ministry, Lamar was a carbon copy of the Campbell adaptation of Common Sense epistemology. "No creed but the Bible." "Read the Bible as if no one had read it before." "Keep your own perspectives out of your reading." "The Bible does not need interpretation"—implying that both mystical and dogmatic theology have strayed. This is orthodox epistemological fare, and Lamar formulated it more systematically than the founder had managed to do.

But Lamar's story is longer than that. Darwinian paradigms and methods were taking over from Baconian approaches in the national intellectual armory of the 1840s. Lamar himself changed, brought himself up to date. Caught up in the late-century spasms reflected in harmonialism, spiritual healing, the strenuous life as ultimately virtuous, and the will to believe, Lamar had moved a great distance by the 1890s. "Vital religion," that is, religion of the heart, had replaced the Campbellian rationalism. The old orthodoxy, wherein the Spirit was constrained by and embedded in the work, converted to a vitalistic force for the new Lamar. Near the end of his life, he shifted again, this time to a form of theistic evolution.

Ideological heritages tend to have a fairly short life span, and Scottish Realism and Newtonian physics are no exceptions. Lamar's own evolution in thought mirrors that human tendency. But the southern Christians, the Churches of Christ, in the words of historians Hughes and Allen, "maintained a milieu supporting Baconianism." Despite later diversification, that brotherhood has perpetuated an affinity for that way of doing religious epistemology.

The Christian movement in the South, thus, has a long history and is not a single stream. Early the O'Kellyite revolution and the Smith-Jones impetus stirred things up among the southern religious, offering alternatives to Methodism and existing forms of Baptist life. Both enterprises have left a legacy, the O'Kelly line most notably and in the national liberal Protestant denomination, the United Church of Christ. A far larger and more influential collection of Christians in the region has been those who embraced the Restorationist platform that appeared in various guises in nineteenth-century America, but definitively in the Stone-Campbell tradition. Since Restorationists could not agree on what exactly was to be restored and how precisely to bring it about, they divided. Southern Restorationists mostly followed the Barton Stone apocalyptic path and took shape in the Churches of Christ, a predominantly southern fellowship. More than a few followed the progressive perspectives of Alexander Campbell to eventuate in the Christian Church (Disciples of Christ) denomination. While strongest in the midwestern states, that body enjoys scattered strength in the South and a considerable presence in central Virginia, central Kentucky, and eastern North Carolina.

These fervent, "new age" Protestant peoples penetrated southern society and culture with their themes and values. But their greatest gifts have been part of the early Americans' quest for freedom. One can almost declare that freedom was their animating spirit. While nearly all the indigenous American Christian movements have allied their new spiritual insights with freedom, none has pursued that goal with the breadth and intensity of the Stone-Campbell tradition.

All these Christians capitalized on the spirit of the liberty Americans fought for and formulated in the Constitution. In the introduction, I touched on the presence of many freedoms that can be identified in the South's religious history, telescoping the list into four clusters of freedom *from*: (1) domination by class, tradition, or both, (2) church, theological system, or both, (3) denial of a people's right to create their own religious life; and (4) constraints of the conventions of polite society.

Since the Christians of the Stone-Campbell movement in particular placed their fingers precisely on the pulse of the national drive toward freedom, treating their history affords an ideal context for a detailed examination. An ideal context, perhaps, but not the only one, for southerners (white citizens, that is) have been declaring freedom throughout their history, sometimes with such effectiveness as to change the course of human history, often in the face of great peril. The eighteenth-century Virginians who led in the framing of the Constitution are nonpareil. The nineteenth-century African Americans are models of courage in the face of systematic denial of freedom. In addition, the record of the region's people in religious liberty is impressive. It extends well beyond the defense of liberty for self and others, admirable as that is, to creativity. Indeed the instinct to create and the capacity for creativity comprise a major theme of this entire study. A number of the freedoms declared reveal a keen sensitivity to democratic principles, others to the theological heritage of the Reformation. Still others respond to the major economic and social transformations characteristic of modern societies. They thus comprise a medley of sacred and secular concerns.

1. Freedom *from* domination by higher social classes of fellow citizens and from tradition in the form of assumptions and conventions that have been handed down and treated as inviolate. Freedom *for* the voices of the ordinary people, really all the people, and for closing out the European-colonial American policy of class hierarchy and religious establishmentarianism. Domination of the lower classes by the genteel, mannered, and sometimes moneyed sectors received its initial heavy blow from Virginia's folk during the late colonial era, with evangelical faith a primary incentive. The instigation for this social-religious revolution arose from

the ranks of the plain people through their congregations newly composed of willful believers. The ancient notion of the church-of-the-realm was challenged and toppled in the process. Establishmentarian policies came in for heavy pounding from the Baptists most forcefully and nowhere with the effectiveness of the new democrats in that state of freedoms, the Old Dominion. The Christian movements followed soon with their assaults on any kind of rule from the top down.

2. Freedom *from* human rational systems, whether organizational or ideological. Freedom *for* the exclusive veracity of Scripture and for the promise of human competence. The Christians score high and consistent on this measure. With great persistence across quite a span, they tackled deeply entrenched notions of how church organization, theological beliefs, and people's roles should be deployed. They opposed creeds and dogmas because they supported the pure and plain meaning of the Bible. They sponsored the individual congregation and each person reading the Bible for herself; this was in preference to any and all institutional arrangements. They depreciated theological systems in favor of discrete biblical passages and teachings. They renounced institutional control and supported lay leadership. They upheld obedience to the Word of God over against man-made forms, measures, and practices. They sought to exchange patriarchy for congregational autonomy and individual responsiveness to the Spirit. Wholeheartedly devoted to human free will, they rejected outright the Calvinist theology of divine election. Au courant in their insistence that Christian people and churches be authentic, they ignored the past, except the normative primordium the contours of which they sought to emulate in the present, predicating that it was possible to do so. Like their Puritan forebears, they labored for the chance to be right (correct) and thus eschewed all social and political constraints. This is indeed an impressive record of accomplishments by the Christians, Baptists, and others. All of

these early Americans practiced democratic liberty, freedom that affords people the chance to take a fresh look, slough off, and reinvent.

3. Freedom *from* slaveowner control, a condition that grew more repressive as social attitudes and laws became increasingly congruent with slaveholders' rights. Freedom *for* worship and for church rule on their own terms. Before emancipation and the end of the Civil War, nearly all black Christians experienced church in a mostly white-fashioned-and-governed setting. Their number huge by the 1860s, black Baptists and Methodists were in position to shape their religious lives to suit themselves. They formed and organized their own congregations, agencies, and eventually denominational structures. Central to this action was the formation of distinctive styles in preaching and music, and even theological formulations. The creativity manifested by African American Christians is probably the single most significant expression of freedom in southern religious history.

4. Freedom *from* restraints on holistic human expression, in spirit, body, and emotions—that is, to pursue the leadings of the heart. Freedom *for* responsiveness to the Holy Spirit. The Christianity of southern black people is one instance of this. The more dramatic and specific example of this freedom occurred when the Spirit Movement issued in Holiness and Pentecostal formations. With these developments around the turn of the twentieth century, the freedom tide reached its highest flow. Now freedom for various forms of external constraint and repression was matched by an accrediting of the power of the inspired heart to give holistic expression. (How this fourth freedom came about historically and what its lineaments were are the subject of chapter 3.)

Two other freedoms that mark the heritage discussed in this book do not quite yield to cluster patterns but are important in the sweep of history and require mention. One is the freedom from division, even from the concept of denominationalism, the freedom for unity. What prescience the early Stone-Campbell disciples unwittingly displayed with reference to the malaise of our era where rivenness is a common condition. Ethnic groups and political factions are hardly living in harmony. Alas, no sector is more tragically fractured than the religious communities.

The other freedom is freedom from uncertainty and skepticism in belief, freedom for trusting some guides to the truth. As complex as this issue is, perhaps we can at least consider that nihilism and absolute relativism are conceptually unnecessary and humanly lethal. The nineteenth-century Christians, and many others, were after something, and on to something. Perhaps we should do a little looking and listening, encouraged by their affirmative spirit.

CHAPTER 3

. . . .

The "of God" Bodies

BETWEEN 1880 AND 1920, a powerful new force appeared on the southern religious scene. By stages and various names, the Holiness and Pentecostal movements burst upon the South, with greatest energy on the slopes of the uplands in lower east Tennessee, northern Georgia, and western North Carolina. The Church of God (of Cleveland, Tennessee), the Church of God in Christ, the Pentecostal-Holiness Church, and the Assemblies of God, along with others, came into being.

All of these claimed that special acts of the Holy Spirit were occurring to individual Christians within congregations newly formed and freshly attuned to God's powerful presence. Hence the term *Spirit Movement* applies; the most popular specific title usage was Church of God.

A student of religion in southern history working thirty or more years ago likely would not have gotten around to including the Pentecostal or Holiness bodies that are present in the region. For not only were they considered religiously strange or weird, or treated as somewhat beneath one's dignity, they also attracted constituencies that fell heavily in the lower social classes, especially with respect to education and influence. No one would have denied their presence in the population, merely shunted them aside as not fully deserving of serious treatment. Moreover, with few exceptions, they had not produced histories of their own movements, and those few were not very professional. All of these conditions now have changed, and with them scholars' perceptions and sense of responsibility.

In addition, the practice of historiography itself has undergone some changes in the last several decades. Doing social history—from the bottom up, is the usual expression for it—has become prominent. But there is another reason for serious historical examination of Pentecostal and Holiness history. These once-excluded religious people are far from that any more. Examples are numerous and well known. I have eagerly, if somewhat timorously, been turning my attention toward them. All of us are greatly helped by extensive historical research accomplished both by insiders and outsiders within the past quarter century. But the most basic datum is that they were "there"; they have been a part of life in the region now for more than a century.

In the introduction and the two previous chapters, I have iterated the freedom theme that has permeated southern religious history and generated much creativity. One aspect of the larger theme is freedom from emotional restraints. One way of characterizing the Pentecostal and Holiness movements has been to note that they freed people to express themselves emotionally. But that is an inadequate way of capturing what the "of God" bodies—more broadly what the Spirit Movements—really stand for. On their own terms, what they insisted on was freedom in the Spirit. It is instructive to note that religious freedoms are never identical with reaction and usually are better than reactive: they are for something as well as from something. If that is not the case, they are probably pathologic.

It is hardly inappropriate or tasteless for a people who celebrate God as near and loving to express that awareness and good news through bodily movements and loud voices. All Christians agree that faith is holistic, in some sense, surely. The churches the first generation of Pentecostal and Holiness people had belonged to (often Methodist) or knew about but were not drawn to, usually suppressed such manifestations.

The time had come for the emerging Spirit Movements to take charge of their own religious destiny. Further, and far more important in their perception of things, the divine Spirit was beckoning, assuring them of his deep yearning to enter and possess their hearts and lives. If the Methodist, Baptist, and other churches would not facilitate the Holy Spirit that they themselves long had talked about, these not-to-be-denied Christians would develop their own channels.

The act of taking matters into one's own hands, taking charge of one's destiny, was already an old pattern in southern religious history. Such a description is pretty apt for what the evangelical Baptists did in Virginia in the mid- to late eighteenth century. No longer would they be dominated and treated condescendingly by the Virginia gentry whom the Anglican Church suited—even if those people of standing had little to do with their movement. The O'Kellyites, the Stoneites, and the Campbellites claimed their places in the sun, although in this case social class was not typically the obstacle they were striving to overcome. Similarly the antimission Baptists would not adjust to the vogue of the times: paying preachers and regarding them as if they were employees; more fundamentally, treating religion as a commodity and churches as superchurches that organize themselves like businesses. In one of the most dramatic developments, the Stoneite Churches of Christ pried apart the Christian movement's classic passion for restoring the primitive church and uniting all Christians in the simple, undenominational Churches of Christ. Restoring came to take precedence over uniting.

In every case, other people and external forces had commandeered the destiny of the devout church men and women who yearned for purity and authenticity. So they got tough, rebelled, caused a stir, and pulled out. Often they called themselves "come-outers." To their minds, of course, it was those others who had pulled out, that is, compromised their faithfulness to a God who made very plain what he expected of his people. In the case of the Spirit Movement of the years before and after 1900, several of them marching under the "of God" banner, only the details differed. The once-dedicated churches that should have known better had given in to newfangled ways that were sure to cool, even chill, the hearts of people earlier aflame with love for the Lord.

The correlation between Holiness and Pentecostal in given bodies is a complex issue. Holiness appeared earlier in the South, in the 1880s. When Pentecostalism emerged around 1905 to 1910, it largely absorbed Holiness, but the former did not discard the latter. In these classic forms, if one were a Pentecostal, that is, had received a "third blessing" of the capacity to "speak in tongues," he or she had already been endued with moral power, the "second blessing," or entire sanctification. Conversion followed by water baptism had already set the Christian apart from the world through the gift of salvation and forgiveness, of course. It is logical to suppose that these miraculous actions of the Holy Spirit were not respecters of gender or race or social class; more than logical, the supposition proves to be factual.[1]

In setting the stage for treatment of these several groups, some external contributing factors must be examined. First, the broadly religiocultural context from which the various Spirit Movements emerged. In the South of the 1890s, with the Civil War three decades past, Reconstruction nearly two decades gone, and Jim Crow laws quickly being passed to secure fixed places for others, the traditional denominations were the Baptist, Methodist, and Presbyterian. All three were overwhelmingly white and all were modernizing, that is, developing extensive area, state, and regional agencies to propagate their work in missions, education, and social ministries. By falling in with the spirit of the times, they had made their peace with the surrounding society and culture; in many respects they *were* the regional society's culture, embodying and fostering its values and perspectives.

The Baptists (of the Southern Baptist Convention) were the sole fellowship that managed to retain a richly diverse social-class composition. This may have had to do with the relative autonomy and local leadership their churches exercised even in the face of expanding central organization. A second factor probably was their ubiquity; they were everywhere, and an incredible diversity accompanied their being situated in towns, cities, farming regions, and mountainous areas, and embracing all the people who lived in all those places. The Presbyterian constituency, rather concentrated in distribution and in ethnic makeup (being largely Scots and Scots-Irish), also swept across a fairly wide socioeconomic range—within those limits. But its people were accustomed to learning, to "doing things decently and in order" and had scarcely tasted anything like "spirit possession." The Methodist Church, it follows, proved the fertile ground for the Spirit Movement. That body too had congregations nearly everywhere, and its heritage fortified it with a keen sense of the "witness of the Spirit." Effervescent occasions such as camp meetings and revivals had been an element in the American Methodist movement, prominently in the South, from its origins in the 1760s.

In the late nineteenth century, an irresistible force met an immovable object. From the one side moved the Wesleyan power of Spirit, the dynamic God working in people's hearts in ways that defied predictability and transcended "reasonable" responses. This collided with the modernization of a Methodism that had honored connectionalism from its earliest times (continuous with its rootage in the Church of England).

The Holiness movement was abroad in the South by the mid-1880s, having begun its penetration of northern Protestants with effect after the Civil War.[2] The natural terrain for its outcropping was the Methodist Episcopal Church, South. Its impact was to come a cropper at the denomination's General Conference of 1894. The language of the bishops' address reveals what was at issue and what produced a stalemate of dissenting proportions: "We do not want an order of pastors to keep up a routine or a higher, freer, bolder order of prophets to bring down fire from heaven. The offering of the regular army is more important than any guerilla warfare, however brilliant." The bishops were spelling out the objection they raised to the initiative for creating an office of evangelist to parallel that of elder and bishop. They sought to reassure holiness sympathizers and all other spiritual Methodists that they remained committed to "holiness of heart and life." But they went on to say that this had its institutional limits. Their address of 1894 condemned the notion of a "holiness party" with its "associations, meetings, and preachers . . . in so far as they claim a monopoly of the experience, practice, and advocacy of holiness, and separate themselves from the body of ministers and elders."[3]

What led to this forthright statement of opposition to Holiness (by contrast with holiness)? John Wesley and classic Methodism had magnified "living a life of victory over sin"—not the same as the teaching of "sinless perfection." The Methodist vocabulary had included a "second work of grace" for a long time, but the denomination saw that experience as part of a process with spiritual growth before and after such a coming-to-awareness, through discipline and self-examination.[4] But by the 1880s in the South—widely in the North two decades earlier—holiness had become Holiness, a conviction that a specific awareness and an experience-event should be constitutive of the higher life, fuller Christian dedication. Identifiable as the experience-event was to their understanding, it was no end in itself, however; it must, and would if authentic, issue in simple, unadorned living and abstinence from worldly ways. Through these developments, the spiritual condition of holiness in a person's life had acquired specificity as to schedule of occurrence and ethical practice. Increasingly this degree of precise characterization became insistent for congregations as well. Of course the truly holy congregations would comprise truly holy people. In addition, churches were to exemplify old-fashioned simplicity, avoiding such superfluities as organs, robed choirs, and ornate buildings. (This is reminiscent of the Stoneite position in the Christian movement coming to the fore about the same time.)

This Holiness movement had attained a kind of institutional standing in the Northeast and Midwest by 1867. It had begun to give full vent to a perfectionist impulse that had been stirring since 1840 or so, with particular effectiveness in Methodism, although never confined to that tradition. The National Holiness Association gained a full head of steam between 1867 and 1883 and came south in the 1870s, here too principally in Methodism (the Methodist Episcopal Church, South). North Georgia emerged as the locus of greatest strength and intensity. The reasons for that geographical concentration are surely multiple, but one is the apparently greater attraction of the Spirit Movements to people of the Appalachian culture—far north Georgia in this case. Another is the stronger connection with the North that obtained within the Unionist sympathizers of the southern highlands area, north Georgia, northwest South Carolina, northeast Alabama, and both slopes of the high mountains between Tennessee and North Carolina. Holiness leadership and forms of expression, in any event, were prevalent in those areas. As the irritation over what to do with its Holiness party increased, the Methodist Church's North Georgia Conference took steps to confine, really isolate, that movement by assigning holiness-oriented preachers to that portion of the state; they set out to "localize the contagion." While the holiness theme in Methodist life could not be contained, the congregations that embraced the holiness manner with such intensity as to turn it into their essential and identifying characteristic continued to be most numerous in that area.[5]

In this book's focus on creativity and diversity, the early southern Holiness developments have high importance. The Methodist (Episcopal, South) Church was hardly a stranger to Wesleyan holiness teaching and expression. But holiness was not widely in favor in the generation before the Civil War, and the war itself played havoc with everything. A face-off was inevitable by the 1880s; it had to do with a creative response to the freedom from-for concern. The modernizing, even bureaucratizing, church was tending toward the proverbial uptown tastes and styles. Also it was tightening its connectionalist heritage. These conditions made three qualities of the budding movement especially troublesome: (1) the independent character of the National Holiness Association—it was national, and thus heavily populated by Yankees; (2) come-outism, best exemplified by Daniel S. Warner, the founder of a new body, the Church of God (Anderson, Indiana); and (3) strange, extreme new doctrines, among them the preaching in some quarters about the "third work of grace" as "fire," abstinence from pork and coffee, and "faith healing."

The church put on the clamps, as the structured Methodist Church had the right to do. Members could practice holiness all they wanted to, but they needed to remain loyal to the body and its traditional demeanor and teachings. The majority remained true to membership requirements, including some holiness-minded congregations. But many left. In doing so they became part of an extremely loose alliance of Holiness churches in the Midwest and the South. A number who had no earlier intention of leaving eventually did so, often with regret. It is estimated that a million Holiness people were so self-identified around 1900. But they were scattered and unorganized by taste and by commitment. Holiness was indeed a movement, but by no stretch one denomination or even ten. In fact, scores of Holiness bodies emerged, the largest being the Church of the Nazarene (itself an amalgam). The title "Church of God" became remarkably standard, more than two hundred choosing that name initially. (Most of them were or became Pentecostal.)

The goal of the new bodies was freedom: in the Spirit; to be led by the Spirit; from sinfulness toward perfection; without any institutional constraints; from the autocracy and ecclesiastical power of the Methodist hierarchy; to be pure groups of pure people, withdrawn from society. Church unity and formal connection with others were of no concern. God in heaven was engaging people on earth, without benefit of clergy; indeed ecclesiastical mediation of any kind was viewed with genuine suspicion.

Mention has been made of the Church of God (Anderson, Indiana). Effectively led by Daniel Warner from 1880, this "of
God" body became and remains the largest—and a paceset-
ting—Holiness denomination. Yet it does not figure prominently in the southern story.[6] The South has not been either its
place of origin or a highly hospitable homeland. Here is a use
of the "of God" title that does not fit in this unfolding history.
Far from univocal, that name points to a good many positions
and emphases. As the South's history advanced, Pentecostalism was to appear, overtake Holiness, join forces with it, and,
for the greater part, absorb it. But the Anderson Church of God
remained Holiness, never embracing Pentecostal doctrine and
practice. As a denomination omitted from this study, it acquires
a kind of privative significance. That is to say, had it emerged as
a forceful regional presence, the whole southern religious historical picture would be different. (Comparable points can be
made about omissions from the Baptist and Christian examina-
tions.) The Anderson church—*that* Church of God—should not
go unremarked, because it illustrates one vital datum in southern religious history: what happened to Holiness, the movement and the concept, in the South. Even casual observers of
the southern religious scene may have noted the greater fre-
quency of "Pentecostal" rather than "Holiness" on church signs
and in listings of religious bodies. I suspect that most southerners suppose the two names are linked, that a group that claims
one of the titles is apt to claim the other, or even that they really
refer to the same phenomenon. In fact, they differ.

Not that the Holiness movement and its denominational
manifestations completely died out in the South. The Church
of the Nazarene grew at a steady pace, mostly in the Midwest,
but by 1916 only about 15 percent of its membership lived in
the southern states, principally in rural areas. The Anderson
Church trailed in the South but claimed some adherents. The
third of the largest Holiness bodies, the Christian and Missionary Alliance, never has managed a widespread presence in the
region.

The relation between Holiness and Pentecostalism, as movements giving rise to denominations and as theological positions, requires further consideration. The two envisionings of God's most authentic church and the higher Christian life are subject to correlation, the Pentecostal-Holiness Church (founded in 1915) standing as the clearest example. Yet holiness is not the same when its setting is Holiness as it is when its setting is Pentecostal-Holiness. All Christians of the holiness persuasion are committed to belief in and practice of a deeply sanctified ("made holy") life. The righteous Lord is able to endue receptive people of faith with the moral power to overcome (in considerable measure) natural human sinfulness: the God who has all power can effect that power within the human heart, soul, and conscience. A spiritual gift—that is what holiness is—of that kind is not necessarily demonstrative. Its essence, its confirmation is in daily living. The act of receiving this gift *may* be accompanied by motor responses, but the contents of the gift are to be lived out, long term. The recipient is sure that God is its author and that she has indisputably received it. But its nature is to point toward actualization.

The Pentecostal experience is demonstrative; in fact, it cannot be nondemonstrative. A critical outsider might brand it phony or showy, an experience that makes one feel good momentarily. But the real issue is the experiencer's perception of it. For him or her, showy it is not, but demonstrative it is by its very nature. This gift of tongues is a public event, and that is all it is. It occurs in the moment and in the presence of others. But these facts do not cheapen it. "In the moment, in public" is its character. One has to move far to another category of understanding to argue that it is, therefore, a flash in the pan, something sporadic or erratic.

The holiness experience and the Pentecostal experience are different kinds of experience. Despite what they share, they are not identical. Their pace is different; their consequentiality is different; their sense of realization is different. For this analysis of the early Holiness and Pentecostal movements in the American South, the notation to be registered is that when they blend, or mix, or seek absorption, something happens to each of the two distinct experiences. Yet holiness is affected more than Pentecostal. The pace and impact of the latter, being demonstrative and public (or else nonexistent), co-opts the former. Holiness may be a single, identifiable, unmistakable experience, but it is inherently of long duration. (At the same time, a Pentecostal experience that is only *of* the moment is no better than showy and a good feeling. If the person who has received the gift of tongues is not holy, then the claimed experience is indeed phony.) May we then expect a higher level of righteousness from Holiness people than from Pentecostal people? Not if the Pentecostal people are to be taken at their word as to their understanding of faithfulness to God. Nevertheless, the two kinds of Spirit experience are different and do not coexist altogether to the enhancement of each.

Holiness as a movement has been less popular and prominent in southern history than Pentecostalism. How did this happen, when Holiness was introduced in the region as early as the 1870s and had acquired a well-distributed following by 1890 or so? The drama of the Holiness movement's lessened impact is heightened by mention of the date 1906, the year in which Pentecostalism in any modern reference came to birth (at the Azusa Street Mission in Los Angeles). How did an adaptation—in certain respects a transformation—follow so quickly on the heels of an innovation? Holiness moved south in the 1880s and was largely absorbed by Pentecostalism that came east from Los Angeles in late 1906.

Historian Vinson Synan summarizes this sweep of events: "Very little of the southern holiness movement remained outside the pentecostal fold . . . after 1907–1908." Enlarging Synan's perspective, historian James Goff points out that in those very earliest days of modern Pentecostalism, "only about half of the established holiness churches in the United States accepted the new Pentecostal doctrine, [but] the percentage was much higher in the southern region."[7] Each geographical subsection of the Pentecostal movement is affected by this development. East of the Appalachians, the Holiness Church of North Carolina, the Fire-Baptized Holiness Church, the Brewerton Presbyterian Church, Holmes Theological Seminary, and the Pentecostal Free-Will Baptist Church all embraced Pentecostalism. So did the Cleveland, Tennessee, Church of God heritage, although it had been only Holiness from the time when A. J. Tomlinson founded it. The same was true of various elements of the western movement that organized as the Assemblies of God in 1915.

Whereas the Holiness movement maintained a strong and independent identity in the North, for the greater part it blended with Pentecostalism in the South and lost some of its specificity. The popular reasoning that the two are one in this region is, thus, more than intelligible, both for historical and lasting reasons. Their apparent commonality traces back for nearly a century. And, in the perception of those with a less explicit commitment to supernaturalism, or none at all, the Holiness experience and the Pentecostal experience may seem indistinguishable. While it would be risky to generalize that wherever the two currents flow together the Pentecostal, so forceful and demonstrative, is likely to give the stream its coloration, that is certainly the case in the American South. For now, the nub of this issue is the power of the Pentecostal phenomenon to attract people to its manner of faith expression and in the early days to wrest them from a new but quite effective Holiness movement.

Three lines of explanation shed some light on this denominational transformation and on the socioreligious context of the turn-of-the-century South. The first is the heritage of revivalism that the Presbyterians had initiated, the Methodists had enlarged and refined, and the Baptists had made their own in the stream flowing from the Great Awakening (1745–70) and the Great Revival (1801–10). This contributed a predilection to regard a direct action of God toward a person as dramatic or event-specific or extraordinary—perhaps even paroxysmic.

While other parts of the country knew such a phenomenon quite well, by the late nineteenth century only the South regarded this as a (or the) standard means of entry into the Christian life. Conversion, as a conscious act of the will, was still seen as necessary, and its occurrence was identifiable by a conversion experience. There is a sense in which the additional experiences or blessings, of tongues, holiness, or both are but an extension of conversion. The ambience of the setting in which the first occurred was replicated in the postconversion "gifts of the Spirit" that came upon a person's life.

The second explanation is the social location of the Pentecostal emergence, namely, in the lower classes in rural areas, mostly quite isolated. The western slope of the Appalachian mountains in lower east Tennessee was one especially fertile home ground. In and near the town of Cleveland, vibrant activity was impossible to overlook. Such existing churches as there were, mostly Baptist and Methodist, were increasingly manifesting marks of the progressivism affecting the region's religious life, as well as its politics and economics. Modernization was extending its clutches to quite remote places. Styles of worship gatherings and ministerial leadership had gone "fancy," thus were less and less suited to local tastes and traditions. The churches now were leaving the people; at least that was the painful, sometimes angry, conclusion of many plain folk in isolated sections of the South. Thus, social class conditions were one decisive factor in the formation of new kinds of churches, Pentecostal ones especially.

A third explanation of the Pentecostal lure is Pentecostalism itself. No matter one's social location—some were economically middle class—Pentecostalism offers something that can be deemed authentically biblical. One does not have to possess a certain temperament to believe that the older churches were not only suppressing emotional expression but also overlooking the first post-Resurrection Pentecost and some Pauline teaching. Why not claim the power patently available to the first generation of Christians? By what hermeneutic principle do Christ's followers of any age decide that what his spirit enabled so long ago in the generation after his ascension had been curtailed or abrogated? The Restorationist Movement so definitive of the Christians, especially Stone-Campbell, had a quality of expectation, optimism, and biblicism. These same elements operated in the American charter three-quarters of a century later among some very plain people who knew nothing about Scottish Realism. Indeed these were not even rationalists. But they had their Bibles open, and they knew perfectly well that God had a simple gift he yearned to give them. In addition, they were heirs of Holiness, a means of understanding God's dealings with his people that magnified the power of his Spirit working within them.

They called this nearness factor "restoring the apostolic faith," or the Latter Rain.[8] Attribute the American penchant for dismissing history to a national character trait, if you will, but the restoration theme is as old as Europe's Protestant Reformation. Pentecostalism is another variant on that theme. This one appeared in the guise of direct experience, the unobstructed flow of the divine spirit into the experience of a company of Christians, in the early days mostly isolated, plain folk. To depreciate the validity of their seeing the effect of this grace in ecstatic forms carries an inherent bias. The case can be made that such a response is an appropriate one for the coming together of a loving God and a redeemed people.

Historian Edith L. Blumhofer is among those who identify Restorationism as one of the roots of American Pentecostalism.[9] (Indeed she gives the title *Restoring the Faith* to her recent study of several aspects of the Pentecostalism movement.) The grounding of that fin de siècle development, however, is remarkably different from the movement that goes by the name Restorationist, the Christians of the Stone-Campbell heritage. The primal elements of earth and air had changed since the heady days of Stone's visions a century earlier and Campbell's a few years later. In the early Republic, the earth was just undergoing settlement as people moved west (not very far) to establish communities and build a society. The time had come to reclaim the ancient for the present, and no obstacles stood in the path of achieving so brilliant a goal. It was less that a new day had dawned than that the primordium had been spied and could be brought forward. Air was clean and clear, unpolluted, in its natural state above the vast farming areas and even above the growing towns and cities. Not surprisingly to the Campbell movement of the near Midwest, the future looked illimitable to church and society alike. So the millennium was dawning for America, not just its Christian identity, but for the entire national life. This was not reform; this was reclamation and reconstruction. Postmillennialism became the only attractive philosophy of the future; Christ would return at the end of a long period of amelioration.

That was Alexander Campbell's take on things. Barton Stone, especially in his southern following, looked out and saw a world that was not and could not be made into the Kingdom of God on earth. Reform would not do. Only divine apocalyptic actions could set things straight. So the Stoneite Churches of Christ—of the southern region from middle Tennessee to Texas—were premillennialists. They looked forward all right, but with hope in the assurance that the high God of heaven would "remove the veil" (apocalypse) when he had brought history to his conclusion. No means of *theirs* could accomplish *his* ends. Along markedly different lines from Campbell, the Stoneite Restorationists also decried reform as their appointed strategy. In truth, they did not subscribe to a strategic notion of God's ways with the world.

The Pentecostals' Restorationism had more in common with the Stoneite Churches of Christ than the Campbellite Disciples of Christ—who essentially shed their radicalism in the flush times of the late nineteenth-century Midwest. Both were pessimistic, from any conventional human perspective. But what characterized Stoneite understanding—rationalism and ecclesiasticism—was of a very different order from Pentecostal thinking. Pentecostals saw the crying need for reform. The churches that once were home were that no more. They had grown cool, lukewarm; they had adapted to progress and development in the allurement of updating and upgrading. Yet the come-outers' agenda soon turned to more positive quests, away from simple reform. They discerned that the Scriptures taught the coming of the Holy Spirit into the midst of and into the individual hearts of the earliest Christians. The constitution of the primitive church (the central Stoneite concern) had little appeal for them. They resisted the denominationalizing tendency that had become so fashionable, and they lamented the moral laxness of the older bodies, deploring the churches' capitulation to worldly customs. But what really excited them was the news of the first Pentecost (fifty days after the first Easter).

On the Pentecostals' scale of values, power outranked propriety; spiritual power lay ahead of formal propriety. Opening their hearts to receive the Spirit overwhelmed them and became the test—"evidence" was their conception of it—of their attunement to God. The distance between heaven and earth had been narrowed, so to speak. Actually the distance had been bridgeable all along; they simply had not discerned the Scriptures deeply and responded with sufficient faithfulness. The untoward ways of the world, including the church in the world, were proving to be God's opportunity for disclosing his truth more fully and unleashing his vast power into their lives in the defining events that followed baptism by water, what they called blessings or works.

It is important to distinguish between Pentecostal then and its current usage by Catholics, Episcopalians, Baptists, and some other Christians, what is more accurately referred to as neo-Pentecostalism. In its original forms in the South, enduement with power to live the higher life (another term for holiness), toward entire sanctification, was of a piece with the gift of speaking in tongues, the Pentecostal experience. That linkage was perfectly natural because in many cases (in the South nearly always) Holiness preceded Pentecostal, and both were acknowledged in the Pentecostal-Holiness bodies. In our own era, the Pentecostal experience is self-contained, that is, not antecedent or subsequent to something like Holiness. It is its own evidence and is self-completing. As in any Christian context, neo-Pentecostal people are meant to practice righteous living. But the experience appears sometimes to come close to being a feel-good occurrence. At its best, it is a tapping of God's power to heal body or mind, to learn the divine will, to nurture love—in general, to signal a deeper dedication to the author of the experience.

Touching on another feature of popular southern religion in the larger setting of American Christianity, observers have wondered why classic evangelicalism has been relatively weak in the South. Regional religious life has only scattered instances of the Dutch Reformed tradition, sectarian Baptist groups, the Mennonite family, and state-church piety communities. None of these branches of Protestantism is angry at society, but all stand somewhat apart from it in values and conventions. The most direct solution to this puzzle concerns ethnicity, a quality tied to immigration. The Northeast, Midwest, and West all received hundreds of thousands of Europeans, which meant, in turn, receiving the sects or denominations they brought with them.

But beyond that, a less immigration-based evangelical heritage, the Holiness, has also not been much of an alternative Christian presence in Dixie, especially compared to the midwestern and northwestern states. Historical investigations illuminate the weakened influence of Holiness as such in a region otherwise profoundly evangelical—but principally with respect to evangelism, that is, generating the conversion experience in the unconverted and unchurched. Holiness as another, and classic, form of evangelicalism would have introduced into the southern stream some missing elements that are abundant in Holiness. That tradition is more disciplined and studious than Pentecostalism; it is also less devoted to evangelism expressed as revivalism. It is more given to dialogue with others and more likely to produce educational and other social institutions that wield influence on the culture.

Pentecostalism must not be stereotyped, of course, but its impact is likely to be local and episodic. Much the same can be said for the new charismatic movements that have gained currency in the South. Both "neo" emergences serve as a soil that nourishes some kinds of fruits more readily than others. The South's indigenous evangelicalism would have been diversified, perhaps made richer, had Holiness and other classic forms been more pervasive.

ONE OF THE IMPRESSIVE aspects of the rise of Holiness and Pentecostalism is their interregional character. Stated differently, these Spirit-driven Christians paid little attention to where they were preaching and calling down the Spirit; even with whom they were fellowshipping. Credentials were important, of course, but for these emphases they had to do with the health of a person's soul, one's energy in the Lord, hardly at all with where he or she called home or what the person's social class was. (That is altogether consistent with Spirit-differentiated religion, but scholars have sometimes overlooked the "religious factor." It is absolutely basic to inquire into what a religious group intends to believe and practice.)

I turn now to the careers of two southern figures to more sharply focus on the Spirit Movement's interregional nature. Joseph H. King helped found the Fire-Baptized Holiness Church—which merged with two other fellowships in 1915 to form the Pentecostal-Holiness Church, one of the three most significant bodies in southern Pentecostalism and in which King held several major offices. From 1898 until his death in 1945 at age seventy-five, King was a veritable Mr. Pentecostal Holiness, which would seem to predict a quite straightforward role. But Bishop King's career had some fascinating turns.[10] To start with, the northwest South Carolina–born King was converted into membership in the Methodist Episcopal (M.E.) Church, South. Later in the same year, 1885, he received an "experience in sanctification." In less than two years' time, the young man applied for a license in the M.E. Church, South, but was turned down—probably because of his strong Holiness sympathies. He was later issued a ministerial license, but a sojourn in Atlanta resulted in his joining a congregation of the Methodist Episcopal Church—meaning "North," but officially without that identifying adjective. His ministry was genuinely underway from this time forward. He graduated from the U. S. Grant University in Chattanooga, Freedmen's Bureau–operated but whose School of Theology was affiliated with the northern Methodist Church.

Over the next five years King left the church of his ordination and joined the Fire-Baptized Holiness Church, a new and rather "quirky" body; served a congregation in Toronto; became an editor for the church in Lincoln, Nebraska; and returned to the north Georgia, northwest South Carolina area as general overseer. All the rest of his career was lived out on a more regular track—but he did travel as a Pentecostal-Holiness Church luminary to Japan, China, the Middle East, and Europe.

The Rev. Joseph H. King is an eddy in a vortex of forces occurring in his part of the South and in burgeoning American evangelicalism in the fin de siècle era. He belonged initially to the southern Methodist Church; next he moved to the northern Methodist Church, which had a strong presence in very few places in the South, most remarkably the old Unionist area of southern Appalachia; then he joined a marginal sect, Fire-Baptized Holiness; finally he became a giant in the leadership ranks of the mainstream Pentecostal-Holiness Church. Ascribing provinciality to him is inaccurate. His contacts and his assignments took him far and near. The particular subsection of the South in which he grew up contributed to that condition; but so also did Pentecostal and Holiness theology, which had (and has) impressively weak reliance on regional culture.

The career of John Lakin Brasher, an important Holiness figure, parallels King's.[11] Born in northeast Alabama in 1868,

Brasher was converted at age thirteen and joined the neighbor-
hood church, the northern Methodist. Like King he graduated
from the School of Theology of the U. S. Grant University in
Chattanooga. Already ordained and preaching from an early
age, he became a Methodist pastor in the young city of Birm-
ingham. His first and second conversion experiences of 1881
and 1886 were brought to fullness in his sanctification experience of 1900.

Now profoundly holiness, he never became Holiness. Indeed
he remained proudly and loyally an ordained minister (elder)
in the Methodist Episcopal Church (North)—the southern and
northern bodies united in 1939—until his death in 1971. He
"traveled 700,000 miles to preach in more than 650 holiness
camp meetings throughout the United States."[12] *Throughout*
captures the generality of his labors; some states in which he
carried on especially productive service were Iowa, Michigan,
New Jersey, and Texas, along with Alabama, Georgia, and Tennessee. Brasher was a national figure in an interregional movement in a sectional (northern) denomination. Even better than
the Pentecostal example, the Holiness movement bespeaks the
capacity of the Spirit Movement to transcend specific cultures.
Holiness never attained widespread popularity in the South,
but some of its national leaders were part of that culture. Regional accents and lore failed to obstruct the holiness ministry.
Along lines illustrated by King and Brasher then, the Spirit
Movement was a national phenomenon, replete with personal
and institutional connections.

To recapitulate this complex history, I refer to James Goff's
three stages of the Pentecostal movement.[13] *Goff's stage 1:* During the 1890s radical holiness groups were breaking with the
church, Methodist principally, and "coming out." These radicals departed from the growing worldliness of the modernizing denominations and embraced purity as souls directly
empowered by the Spirit. This pattern of change was prominent in the South of that decade and the next, particularly in

North Carolina and Tennessee. This is the theater in which Joseph H. King, the Fire-Baptized Holiness Church, and the northern Methodist Church performed important roles.

Goff's stage 2: From a highly unlikely pouring out of the Spirit in 1906 gushed unquenchable appetites for more, indeed for the practice of Spirit-dominated church life. Why highly unlikely? Because this epochal event took place in an obscure mission in Los Angeles, at Azusa Street. Far from standing as a local phenomenon, this revival soon turned into a national event. Christians from the Midwest and the South arrived by train to see what wondrous things the Holy Spirit was accomplishing. Among those providing leadership from the beginning was William J. Seymour of Louisiana and Texas, a black holiness preacher who had suffered some exclusion in his home areas (and even on the train going to California).[14] He was a principal figure at the southern California revival. The word circulated in the national Holy Spirit communities and drew in a sizable contingent of southern Holiness people. One was Aubrey J. Tomlinson of Cleveland, Tennessee; another was G. B. Cashwell of eastern North Carolina. The effect of Azusa on the infant Cleveland Church of God movement proved to be transformative. What had been Holiness only now embraced Pentecostalism, forever stamping that heritage with the doctrine of tongues.

The Cashwell story is more dramatic than Tomlinson's. From a profoundly race-conscious area of the traditional South, Cashwell boggled at being "under" a Negro, but he brought the issue to prayer and underwent a kind of conversion. He also converted to Pentecostalism, from his previous stance as only Holiness. Taking his new awareness back home, he wrought mighty things among a people already committed to Spirit doctrines and probably suggestible to more, but not yet specifically to tongues.[15] It is another of the curiosities of southern religious history that a tiny mission in far away Los Angeles became the rallying center for a national movement that included these plain-folk developments in a region that was doing as little interacting as possible in matters religious as well as political-economic. That is to say, with the exception of Holiness and Pentecostal, where putting the Holy Spirit first relegated social and cultural issues, such as regional self-consciousness and exclusivism, to the periphery.

The southern Spirit churches were interracial from the inception of the movement to 1912 or so in the Cleveland body, and somewhat later in others. However, the signal story concerning southern blacks rests in their own black church denominations. Two of the travelers from afar at Azusa were Charles Harrison Mason and C. P. Jones, black preachers from Memphis. Already won over to Holiness (from Baptist), they had recently formed the Church of God in Christ (COGIC) (now, incidentally, the largest Pentecostal denomination and the second largest black denomination in the United States). What took place at Azusa Street accomplished much healing and reconciling. At the same time, it generated differences. Both Mason and Jones believed in the experience of baptism with the Holy Spirit. Jones was convinced of the reality of a third work of grace that "complete[d] the believer in Christ" and resulted in power manifested in effective service, the heart of the Holiness program. But Mason embraced the Pentecostal message, announcing upon his return to Memphis that "the Holy Spirit had taken full control of me." Because Jones could not accept the new message—he did regard it as "new"—the two parted company. Jones's party formed the Church of Christ, Holiness and disfellowshipped those who advocated tongues. With regard to growth in numbers, the future lay heavily with Mason's Pentecostal church, currently 4.5 million members strong; Jones's stabilized around 100,000. COGIC remained interracial until the 1920s, a rather lengthy stretch considering racial attitudes in that era.[16]

Goff's stage 3: This final step in Pentecostal denominational formation centers on the splits that occurred in the young bodies, that between Mason and Jones being one of them. A particularly disputatious split occurred in Cleveland. In 1914, founder A. J. Tomlinson was elected general overseer in the Church of God for life. As the next few years passed, power for disbursing the Church of God's funds became more centralized and therefore at Tomlinson's discretion. This policy aroused a great deal of opposition, and in 1923 the historic single body split into two, the Church of God (Cleveland, Tennessee) and the Tomlinson Church of God. The latter name held for a decade after Tomlinson's death in 1943, since which time it has been known as the Church of God of Prophecy. These naming words, "of Prophecy," are significant. This thirty-year-old body with a new name was nothing new; the members knew full well that this was God's church in line with the message of the biblical prophets.[17] But even these Spirit-driven Christians could not escape the factiousness that seems inevitably to follow human aspirations of all kinds.

These "of God" bodies, different as they were, and even when they were at odds with each other, manifested a fairly uniform attitude toward the ways of the world. They were come-outers in more ways than one, from social-behavioral conventions as well as from the older established denominations. They vociferously opposed the entire "liquor traffic." That meant they must have nothing to do with making it, marketing it, or consuming it. Of course they were ardent prohibitionists; yet, it did not follow from this commitment that they participated in the public political activities that led to the Eighteenth Amendment. These seekers of higher righteousness had their principles. From there the moral codes were apt to vary somewhat between groups. Some stridently opposed showy costumery for women. The wearing of jewelry was condemned, as was fine dress generally and clothing one's self in skimpy apparel. Strict observance of the Sabbath characterized all of them. In some, a strong anti–secret society animus prevailed. This included, interestingly, the Ku Klux Klan, all Masonic orders, and labor unions. Secret they all were not, but all were exclusive, a trait these populist democratarians held as contrary to God's law.[18]

Some were pacifist, most openly the Cleveland Church of God. Historian Mickey Crews's research reveals how extensive their argumentation for pacifism was. War was not a righteous cause, hence could not be countenanced by Christians who sought to live by the Spirit and were assured that they had entered the third state of grace. At the level of public policy, they stood foursquare in opposition to a declaration of war, and what they saw as its corollary, the draft. As basic a teaching as any was their conviction that the end-time was near. It is that world-changing event that God's people should point to, leaving alone man-made efforts of any kind, especially any as destructive as war. There is a war to be waged, to be sure, but it is the Lord's against the forces of wickedness and faithlessness.

As a mark of the Cleveland body's gradual accommodation to conventional society, the church experienced some softening of its antipacifism stand with America's entry into World War I. In the 1930s, their idealistic hopes for the nation's noninvolvement in the gathering storm faded. By 1941, the attitude had shifted to that of being cooperative. Patriotism had come to be interpreted as participating in the war effort in numerous ways. Many of the men in the church were drafted, some volunteered. (This evolution, incidentally, took place in the Churches of Christ also. That brotherhood once truly sectarian, a condition reflected as well by its pacifist stance as anything, had begun to take on some of the qualities of a denomination.)

The place of women in these early Spirit communities of faith is instructive. Women had been members and testifying speakers in the church congregations from the beginning. Specifically in the Church of God (Cleveland), women had been preaching from the pulpit since 1907. But ordination was not an office open to them following formal action taken by the general assembly in 1909. They continued to preach, nevertheless, and they were certified as foreign missionaries from that season on.

Their work in orphanages and as teachers in children's classes had always been treasured.[19]

It is generally maintained that the three major Pentecostal traditions that arose in the South are the Pentecostal Holiness, the Church of God in Christ, and the Church of God (Cleveland, Tennessee).[20] A fourth group worthy of listing in this study in southern history, certainly because of its size, is the Assemblies of God (AOG). The reason for excluding it from the top three is its geographical marginality, being as much midwestern as southern, and when southern principally southwestern. But there is nothing minor or peripheral about the Assemblies of God, whether the perspective is regional or national. In fact, if this were a book about broadly American denominations, the AOG would rival all three main southern branches in size, distribution, and influence.

The Assemblies came into being in 1914 without any intention of succumbing to the usual propensity for forming another sect or denomination.[21] (That is a story we have run across before.) Actually the body was a confederation of many independent congregations. This is significant in seeming to mark the arrival of a new stage in the American modernizing process that hardly any institutions, even sectarian ones, could avoid. Also it reflects some evolution in Pentecostals' common life. In the slightly earlier, related development of Pentecostalism in the true South of Georgia, the Carolinas, and Tennessee, a different pattern had prevailed. There the movement affected already existing bodies by introducing them to a new doctrine.

At the founding council in Hot Springs, Arkansas, these Pentecostals spoke earnestly of unity (another repetition in southern religious history), of all God's people taking on God's business together. They sought diligently to avoid potentially divisive creeds. Wearing a seamless garment proved too much, however. Within a few years the AOG had added one more to the list of independent bodies informed by a keen sense of identity. They yearned to be one, but also distinctive. Nevertheless, the Assemblies were indistinguishable from the other young Spirit groups in registering a protest against modernity. They rejected basing life on reason or science, instead positing the reality of a God who can be known in the experience of any person and responded to. This body in particular has struggled quite self-consciously to keep in balance charisma and institution. That is to say, the AOG has organized for service and education, but it has sought to await the Spirit's leading in order to avoid relying on modern modes of group life. Like most other Pentecostals, they have been quite reluctant to participate directly and actively in the political arena.

Two other conditions that sooner or later affected the various Pentecostal formations hit home with the AOG too. One was unity, the other race, and they were—of course—intertwined. The new Assemblies' fellowship soon had to face the "Oneness theology" dispute. Some began to insist that baptism in the Spirit was in the name of Jesus *only*, not Father, Son, and Spirit, there being only one personality in the Godhead. Perhaps the Restorationist impulse was operating here; they strove to be New Testament people in a quite empirical sense. Postbiblical church Trinitarian formulations went beyond the Bible. In any event they were a "Jesus people" (to employ a term in recent usage in charismatic circles). Threeness versus Oneness may have seemed to others a fruitless and diverting argument, but it was real within the Assemblies' fellowship (and was inherited by the council formed in 1914).[22]

Three principal Oneness sects appeared. One comprised black congregations only, the Apostolic Overcoming Holy Church of God. A second, the Pentecostal Assemblies of Jesus Christ, was very largely white; through a later merger it became the United Pentecostal Church, now the largest "unitarian Pentecostal denomination." The third, the Pentecostal Assemblies of the World, centered in Indianapolis, was deeply interracial until 1924 when black leadership took charge; the body remains principally a black denomination.

The theme established at the beginning of this treatment of the "of God" bodies, and the Spirit Movement more generally, was freedom *from* and freedom *for*. Even in this brief treatment, it is possible to discern the overthrowing of old restrictions and bonds. The Holiness and Pentecostal people opened up and allowed the powerful Spirit of God to enter their lives, with moral enduements and Spirit possessions. In the process they had to leave the older bodies, either by choice or by exclusion, to create their own congregations and institutions, some highly, some loosely organized. That new condition of life cost them some anguish, but they knew what they were doing and have persisted. Their numbers have become great, approaching 10 million, and their influence far more extensive even than their own membership rolls. Any effective treatment of the variety of religious movements in the American South includes them prominently and is bound to trace out their origins, their messages and positions, and their impact on the culture: freedom *from* humanly imposed restraint, freedom *for* claiming the divine Spirit in their lives and the world around us all.

CHAPTER 4

Interpretation
and Conclusion

I HAVE EXAMINED three prominent Protestant name groups in the American South: the Baptists, the "Christians," and the "of God" bodies. Further, within each cluster I have considered several "eaches" that identify themselves by the cluster's common name. To what extent do these three particular religious units afford insight and understanding concerning southern religious history, and by extension the general history of the South? How do they look when one tries to coordinate and correlate them? Does this selection and treatment offer fresh interpretation, or at least a slightly different perspective on the life of a people, culture, and society? What can be learned about the whole by considering all three together? I see four major transitions, shifts, turning points, or new directions in southern religious history, which, while not confined to the nineteenth century, devolve upon that momentous era, or take place within it, or evolve from it.

The first occurred in the period 1740 to 1790 when the old religious establishment was toppled. The ancient European (and colonial American) policy of one-church-for-one-society was challenged and had to yield. The legal and fiscal arrangement favoring one church over all others (sometimes, if some had their druthers, excluding all pretenders) gave way to the religious ways of the common folk. Gentility, prestige, and tradition surrendered to Baptist and Methodist people and styles and forms. Thus, in the late colonial and early republican decades, a new indigeneity replaced the old establishment.

The second transition came to climax in the 1830s with the informal, unofficial "establishment" of the many folk formations that had altered public policy earlier. The Baptists and Methodists emerged as dominant in this second establishment. They did not do so in legal or fiscal respects but rather by becoming the approved center and standards-maker of the society's religious life. If a Christian community did not manifest the evangelical position and manner of these active groups, its constituency was viewed as a quasi-ethnic group. I contend that we do not tamper with accuracy in speaking of the transference from one establishment to another, from de jure to de facto.

The third transition, occurring in the thirty years following emancipation and the Civil War, is the formation of separate and independent black churches and denominations. Black people, the great majority enslaved, had been part of biracial congregations and had developed endogamous Christian religious rituals and styles. Now, presented with opportunity and necessity, they constructed black Baptist and Methodist churches. This change generated tremors in the older churches (now all white) and brought into existence a major new social institution—one wonders how many could see that at the time.

The fourth transition occurred in the years just before and after 1900 when another folk sector took its religious destiny into its own hands. The Holiness and Pentecostal movements erupted among some very plain people. Perceiving that both they and the divine Spirit were being left out by the churches that had been in cultural control since the informal establishment dating from the 1830s, now increasingly institutionalized, they pulled out and started their own churches.

The flow of the history of these four periods makes for a dramatic story. One aspect is the freedom theme developed in chapter 2. Each period represents a determination to be free *from* something that constrains, *for* something expansive and authentic. Equally significant, however, is the message they all reflect: discontinuity in the religious life of the people of the American South. Most of us who studied this subject in the early years of the recovery of southern religious history—especially a few venerables like me—erred in claiming virtual continuity from the late colonial season to the present. We were enticed to that view by the persistence of the evangelical heritage and by the relative homogeneity of the regional population when a demographic revolution was unsettling the rest of the country.

It is true that changes are harder to discern here than in the America to the north where Jews and Catholics appeared in huge numbers to make everything different; also appearing were ethnic Protestants and "new religions" both imported and homegrown. The South's span of disruption and change has been decidedly narrower, to be sure. But citizens and social leaders in Mississippi, Virginia, and elsewhere trembled at the quakes shaking their 'foundations. "What are we to do with all these new problems?" was about as frightening in Virginia in the 1760s as in Boston in the 1840s, in Alabama in the 1870s as in western Pennsylvania simultaneously. One might argue that little of the South's change has been glamorous, progressive, or modern. But disruption and dislocation have been endemic to regional life. Pain, risk, uncertainty, and damaging consequences have bored deep into human sensibility in the more conservative, less progressive region, as they have everywhere else.

DOWN TO CASES. Baptists, arriving the earliest of the three illustrative clusters, have been party to every transition or shift that has characterized the South's religious and sociocultural history. They, along with Presbyterians and Methodist Anglicans, engineered the revivals of 1745 to 1770, principally through their Separates variant. They and the Methodists led the plain folks' evangelical revolt against the policy of religious establishment. Manners, conventions, and rights of birth and ownership ceased to animate church life; instead, inner piety and God-awareness, plus disciplined living, were taken to constitute it properly. They were in the vanguard of the "transformation of Virginia." Similarly, they (in league with Methodists) were out in front in the second establishment. They had become socially influential, even powerful, by the 1830s. At the most basic level, their way of doing Christianity's business became representative of the popular religion of the region. The Southern Baptist Convention became the religious version of "America's team" in 1845.

The Baptist name-group outdid itself in the third transition that wielded such power in the years after emancipation and the Civil War. Black Baptists, that is, for Baptists these newly freed men and women were. They had been introduced to the heritage by caring and concerned, and guilt-ridden and social control–minded, white Baptists. Soon the heritage became their own. They stood poised to continue, now on their own terms, once opportunity and necessity greeted them.

Baptist participation in the fourth transition was the smallest and the least positive, but the Landmark program has been a factor in white Baptist life ever since. As the heritage underwent modernization, it left behind the poorer classes, especially in the Carolinas and east Tennessee, thus inviting the rise of the new sectarian Spirit bodies. More of the come-outers forsook Methodist churches than Baptist, but both were widely judged to have turned modernist, or highfalutin.

Other branches of the Baptist cluster played different roles, displaying the classical sectarian face of that once radical, and rarely altogether accommodating, Protestant group. The Primitive Baptists recoiled from the very earliest Baptist cooperative activities, from the formation of missionary societies, and from paid clergy and organized denominational life. Those institutional trends helped bring about the second establishment, a condition the Hard Shells predicted with alarm before the cen-

tury's middle third and had nothing to do with once their pre-
dictions had come true. During the same stage of regional history, the Landmarkists declared a plague on both fellow Baptists' houses, even denying that either one had drawn a bead
on what Baptistism stood for. The only genuine church being a
local Baptist one, all churches that flirted with institutional cooperation among themselves, or with other so-called Christians (of whatever ilk), discredited themselves in the process.
What the Landmarkists began in the second transition period,
they perpetuated in the fourth, becoming the Baptist sample of
the come-outer convictions that prompted the Spirit bodies to
declare their freedom from the modernizing denominations.
The battle cry of the Baptist plain folk was authenticity, however, not unrestrained responsiveness to the Spirit (as with the
"of God" people).

The "Christian" movement emerged in the years following
the first transition period. The earth having been successfully
turned by the eighteenth-century dissenters from establishment, they took advantage, enlarging the practice of Christian
liberty. The O'Kelly people, first Republican Methodists and
later the Southern Christian Conference, threw off centralized
government beginning in the 1790s. Never truly separatist
or purist in their aims, they took on denominational trappings
during the season of the second establishment, to which they
were a kind of co-lateral partner. They continued on that course,
insisting on congregational and biblical authority unimpeded
by mediating structures. Their cooperative spirit made them a
candidate for national ecumenical participation in the twentieth century.

The Stone-Campbell version of the Christian movement
sailed through somewhat heavier seas. It too was heir to the
first transition's effective work. In celebrating freedom from all
creeds, systems of thinking, and institutional means to ends, it
exalted the facts of the Gospel in Scripture. Its more adaptive
sector, the Disciples, descendants of the spirit of the later
Alexander Campbell, were caught up in the second establish-

ment of the South, and even more prominently in the midwestern manifestations of protoecumenical American Protestantism. In the preceding decade or two, however, it had rectified more than it recruited, aggressively proselytizing sheep from other folds to set them on the straight path. The more liberal Stone-Campbell followers, the Disciples of Christ, failed to feel many of the tremors of the South's third and fourth transitions.

The Stoneite heritage, so vigorous in the middle South, developed a sectarian personality. Sects, by their nature, stand sufficiently apart from general cultural ebbs and flows so that they notice them little and are not swept along by them. The Stoneites' apocalyptic worldview lifted them above most worldly conditions. Resisting the lures of the second establishment was their stock-in-trade. Less active in opposing segregation than they had been in supporting abolition, they missed the convulsions of the third transition. They participated in the fourth, in an aberrant way, using the come-outer, sectarian spirit of the age to go public with their already effectual separation from the more liberal Disciples. To my knowledge, no sect of the South has enjoyed as long and successful a life as the Stone-influenced Churches of Christ. (It remains arguably sect-like to our time, but not without several denomination-like characteristics for most of this century.)

The "of God" bodies define the fourth transition. Saying that is almost sufficient. They virtually missed out on the first three. But their embodiment was the gleam in the eyes of the parental Methodists who had lived by the "witness of the Spirit" since Oxford and Aldersgate in the 1730s. What they heralded was ancient and now being restored. The offspring appeared only because the parents had forsaken the birthright. At any rate, that was the way they saw it. Moreover, having missed out on the third transition, they proceeded to live it out by being interracial early and later spawning the Spirit Movement's own black denominations.

How are the three name-groups coordinated? The three entered the culture at different times, at successive stages in the

unfolding development of life in the region, and each underwent significant changes. In such ways, they help define the
course of southern religious history. There are no neat and
tidy patterns; history seldom offers those. With respect to their
functions in the long sweep of regional history, they arose to
address particular questions and issues and provided the entire southern heritage with a glossary of religious terms and a
distinctive time line.

The Baptists popularized revivals as the means of bringing the unchurched—the lost, or unsaved—into the Christian
life. *Entry*, with emphasis on the moment of entry, has been
a major Baptist concern and contribution to the regional religious repertoire. The "Christians" responded to God's calling
to set the church(es) on the straight path to true normativity, by
restoring the primitive church. Theirs has been the responsibility of describing, making the case, arguing, and debating. In
fact, debates and lectures have been a prominent and fitting
technique to fulfill their function. The "of God" impetus came
into being to *empower* the already believing. Their message,
often presented in camp meetings or revivals, was that conversion and water baptism are only the beginning of the Christian's relationship to God. His most glorious flowers only
grow at the highest elevation, where the person opens up and
yields to the Holy Spirit who endues one with spiritual gifts,
centrally the capacity to speak in tongues.

The groups may have chosen to relate to each other, inside
the name-group or with the other two clusters. Or they may
have chosen isolation, to a greater or lesser degree. No matter
the course pursued, they have been coimplicated in the stream
of southern history. They have participated in that history
as major factor, element, initiator, and consequence. At some
times reactive, at others adventurous, they have always been
creative. Their normative sources have impelled them, usually
reining in the routes they might choose. The conditions around
them have elicited their responses, sometimes to reject, at
other times to embrace, or to enlarge.

Earlier I sought to describe the evangelical spirit in such phrases as "always wanting more," "never quite settled in," "never getting enough" of purity, authenticity, and normativity. Baptist Christians, "Christian" Christians, and "of God" Christians continue the South's two-and-a-half-century heritage of religious vibrancy, taking much from it and giving plenty back, always deeply a part of it. Variety has been common, freedom has generated more freedom, and creativity has produced fresh forms. Perhaps those factors help account for the high proportion of religious intensity in the lives of the region's people.

Notes

INTRODUCTION

1. One fine, quite recent illustration of such a study is found in Paul W. Harvey, "Southern Baptists and Southern Culture, 1865–1920," (Ph.D. diss., University of California, Berkeley, 1992). Harvey is referring to Baptists in the South rather than members of the Southern Baptist Convention only.

2. John B. Boles, "The Discovery of Southern Religious History," *Interpreting Southern History*, ed. John B. Boles and Evelyn Nolen (Baton Rouge: Louisiana State University Press, 1987).

3. Donald G. Mathews, "'Christianizing' the South" (typescript, 1994), used by permission.

4. Quoted in David Edwin Harrell, Jr., *The Social Sources of Division in the Disciples of Christ, 1866–1900* (Atlanta: Publishing Systems, 1973), 330–31.

5. Nathan O. Hatch, *The Democratization of American Christianity* (New Haven: Yale University Press, 1989).

CHAPTER 1: THE BAPTISTS

1. Walter B. Shurden, "The Southern Baptist Synthesis: Is It Breaking?" *Baptist History and Heritage* 16 (April 1981): 2–19.

2. William L. Lumpkin, *Baptist Foundations in the South* (Valley

Forge, Penn.: Judson Press, 1963). This interpretive study also points to primary sources.

3. Leon McBeth, *The Baptist Heritage* (Nashville: Broadman Press, 1987), and Robert A. Baker, *The Southern Baptist Convention and Its People, 1607–1972* (Nashville: Broadman Press, 1974), are two general studies that treat the sweep of the history of the Baptists in the South.

4. Byron Cecil Lambert, *The Rise of the Anti-Mission Baptists* (New York: Arno Press, 1980), 135–50.

5. William L. Lumpkin, "Separate Baptists," in *Encyclopedia of Religion in the South*, ed. Samuel S. Hill (Macon, Ga.: Mercer University Press, 1984), 685.

6. Rhys Isaac, *The Transformation of Virginia, 1740–1790* (Chapel Hill: University of North Carolina Press, 1982).

7. I am indebted to James Mathis, Ph.D. student in history at the University of Florida, for facts and insights concerning the Primitive Baptists.

8. Lambert, *Anti-Mission Baptists*, preface, 23–114.

9. Cushing B. Hassell, *History of the Church of God from the Creation to AD 1885: Including Especially the History of the Kehukee Primitive Baptist Association* (Middletown, N.Y.: Gilbert Beebe's Sons, 1886), 739.

10. Bertram Wyatt-Brown, "The Antimissionary Movement in the Jacksonian South: A Study in Regional Folk-Culture," *Journal of Southern History* 36 (February 1970): 528–29.

11. During the days of my Averitt Lectures in Statesboro, Georgia, Dr. Averitt, the benefactor, took me on a tour of Primitive Baptist churches in that town and in nearby communities. My eyes flew wide open upon seeing the world's largest Primitive Baptist church and observing how modern the building and organization are.

12. For a detailed study of the Landmark Baptist movement, see James E. Tull, *A History of Southern Baptist Landmarkism in the Light of Historical Baptist Ecclesiology* (New York: Arno Press, 1980).

13. Ibid., 626.

14. Richard T. Hughes and C. Leonard Allen, *Illusions of Innocence: Protestant Primitivism in America* (Chicago: University of Chicago Press, 1988), 94.

15. For an extensive treatment of the history of black churches in the South between 1865 and 1900, see William E. Montgomery, *Under Their*

Own Vine and Fig Tree: The African-American Church in the South, 1865–1900 (Baton Rouge: Louisiana State University Press, 1993).

16. C. Eric Lincoln and Lawrence H. Mamiya, *The Black Church in the African American Experience* (Durham, N.C.: Duke University Press, 1990), 242–46.

17. Joseph R. Washington, Jr., "The Peculiar Peril and Promise of Black Folk Religion" in *Varieties of Southern Evangelicalism*, ed. David Edwin Harrell, Jr. (Macon, Ga.: Mercer University Press, 1981), 61.

18. For a treatment of Holsey's theology, see Edward L. Wheeler, *The Black Minister in the New South, 1865–1902* (Lanham, Md.: University Press of America, 1986), 44–45. Glenn T. Askew has traced Holsey's remarkable career in "Black Elitism and the Failure of Paternalism in Postbellum Georgia: The Case of Bishop Lucius Henry Holsey," *Journal of Southern History* 58 (November 1992): 637–66.

19. Margaret Washington Creel, *"A Peculiar People": Slave Religion and Community Culture among the Gullahs* (Albany: State University of New York Press, 1988).

20. William R. Glass, "The Development of Northern Patterns of Fundamentalism in the South, 1900–1950," (Ph.D. diss., Emory University, 1991).

21. The original version of this history of the Bob Jones phenomenon is contained in Mark Taylor Dalhouse, *Bob Jones University and the Shaping of Twentieth-Century Separatism* (Athens: University of Georgia Press, forthcoming).

CHAPTER 2: THE "CHRISTIANS"

1. Durward T. Stokes and William T. Scott, *A History of the Christian Church in the South* (Elon College, N.C., 1973), 25–34, passim. See also Charles Franklin Kilgore, *The James O'Kelly Schism in the Methodist Episcopal Church* (Mexico City: Casa Unida de Publicaciones, 1963), 5–33.

2. Byron Cecil Lambert, *The Rise of the Anti-Mission Baptists* (New York: Arno Press, 1980), v, chap. 1.

3. Ibid., 35.

4. Ibid., 89, 97.

5. For the nineteenth-century history of the Stone-Campbell Christian movement, I have relied heavily on three studies: David Edwin

Harrell, Jr., *Quest for a Christian America: The Disciples of Christ and American Society to 1866*, vol. 1 (Nashville: Disciples of Christ Historical Society, 1966); Harrell, "Religious Pluralism: Catholics, Jews, and Sectarians," in *Religion in the South*, ed. Charles Reagan Wilson (Jackson: University Press of Mississippi, 1985), 59–82; and Richard T. Hughes, *Reviving the Ancient Faith: The Story of Churches of Christ in America* (Grand Rapids, Mich.: William B. Eerdmans, 1996). Many other books and essays treat the larger tradition, often with a tilt in favor of developments in the North. These three are invaluable for working with the movement's history in the South, which means principally the Churches of Christ.

6. See Hughes, *Reviving the Ancient Faith*. See also Michael W. Casey, "From Pacifism to Patriotism: The Emergence of Civil Religion in the Churches of Christ during World War I," *Mennonite Quarterly Review* 66 (July 1992): 376–90.

7. Cushing B. Hassell, *History of the Church of God from the Creation to AD 1885: Including Especially the History of the Kehukee Primitive Baptist Association* (Middletown, N.Y.: Gilbert Beebe's Sons, 1886), 739.

8. Harrell, *Quest*, viii. For one taxonomy of contemporary Churches of Christ diversity, see J. Gordon Melton, *The Encyclopedia of American Religions*, vol. 2 (Tarrytown, N.Y.: Triumph Books, 1991), 99–102.

9. Kilgore, *O'Kelly Schism*, 5–6, 20, 29.

10. Stokes and Scott, *Christian Church*, 26; Charles C. Ware, *Barton Warren Stone* (St. Louis: Bethany Press, 1932), 147.

11. Kilgore, *O'Kelly Schism*, 33.

12. Stokes and Scott, *Christian Church*, 41.

13. D. Newell Williams, "Springfield Will and Testament," in *Encyclopedia of Religion in the South*, ed. Samuel S. Hill (Macon, Ga.: Mercer University Press, 1984), 732–33.

14. Hughes, *Reviving the Ancient Faith*.

15. Ibid.

16. Ibid.

17. Ibid.

18. Harrell, *Quest*, 53.

19. Harrell, "Religious Pluralism," 324–25.

20. Hughes, *Reviving the Ancient Faith*. In his first chapter, Hughes contends that the Churches of Christ "sect" can be traced to the 1840s.

21. In *Quest for a Christian America*, Harrell contends that while instrumental music did not become a major issue until after the Civil War, it carried symbolic significance much earlier.

22. David Edwin Harrell, Jr., *The Social Sources of Division in the Disciples of Christ, 1866–1900* (Atlanta: Publishing Systems, 1973), 335–56.

23. Quoted in Harrell, *Social Sources*, 330–31.

24. Harrell, *Social Sources*, 97.

25. Ibid., 106–28.

26. Ibid., 112–13.

27. Ibid., 106.

28. Lester G. McAllister and William E. Tucker, *Journey in Faith: A History of the Disciples of Christ* (St. Louis: Bethany Press, 1975), 190–94. See also Hughes, *Reviving the Ancient Faith*.

29. Richard T. Hughes and C. Leonard Allen, *Illusions of Innocence: Protestant Primitivism in America* (Chicago: University of Chicago Press, 1988), 119, 120, 124, 132.

30. Ibid., 132.

31. Don Haymes, "Lectureships (Churches of Christ)," in *Encyclopedia of Religion in the South*, 401–402.

32. Hughes and Allen, *Illusions of Innocence*, 149.

33. Samuel S. Hill, "Campbell-Stone on the Frontier: The Only Ones Weren't the Only Ones," in *Lectures in Honor of the Alexander Campbell Bicentennial, 1788–1988* (Nashville: Disciples of Christ Historical Society, 1988), 65–78.

34. Hughes and Allen, *Illusions of Innocence*, 153–69.

CHAPTER 3: THE "OF GOD" BODIES

1. Vinson Synan, *The Holiness-Pentecostal Movement* (Grand Rapids, Mich.: William B. Eerdmans, 1971), 15–16, 31, 46–48.

2. Ibid., 39.

3. J. Lawrence Brasher, *The Sanctified South: John Lakin Brasher and the Holiness Movement* (Urbana: University of Illinois Press, 1994), 37–40.

4. Synan, *Holiness-Pentecostal*, 19.

5. Ibid., 37, 50.

6. Ibid., 46, 59, 79–80.

7. Ibid., *The Old-Time Power: A History of the Pentecostal Holiness Church* (Franklin Springs, Ga.: Advocate Press, 1973), 115. See also

James R. Goff, Jr., "The Pentecostal Catalyst to the South: G. B. Cashwell (1906–1908)" (typescript, 1980) used by permission.

8. James R. Goff, Jr., *Fields White unto Harvest: Charles F. Parham and the Missionary Origins of Pentecostalism* (Fayetteville: University of Arkansas Press, 1988), 62–63.

9. Edith L. Blumhofer, *Restoring the Faith: The Assemblies of God, Pentecostalism, and American Culture* (Urbana: University of Illinois Press, 1993), 3, 4–5, introduction.

10. King's career can be traced in his autobiography, Bishop Joseph H. King, *Yet Speaketh: Memoirs* (Franklin Springs, Ga.: Publishing House of the Pentecostal Holiness Church, 1949). The historian's refinement of that episodic presentation can be found in David A. Alexander, "Bishop J. H. King and the Emergence of Holiness Pentecostalism," *Pneuma* 8 (fall 1986): 159–83.

11. A most effective study of Brasher is that written by a grandson. See Brasher, *The Sanctified South*. This book illuminates holiness, the Holiness Movement, and the style of holiness preaching, as well as Brasher's career.

12. Ibid., xi.

13. Goff, *Fields White unto Harvest*, 6–7.

14. Seymour's impact is treated by a number of historians. See especially Blumhofer, *Restoring the Faith*, 55–60; Goff, *Fields White unto Harvest*, 107–20; and Synan, *Holiness-Pentecostal*, chap. 5.

15. Goff, "Pentecostal Catalyst."

16. Mason, Jones, and the origins of the Church of God in Christ have not yet received adequate treatment in the literature. But see Blumhofer, *Restoring the Faith*, 73–74, for a pertinent discussion. For a full-length study, see James Oglethorpe Patterson, German R. Ross, and Julia Mason Atkins, eds., *History and Formative Years of the Church of God in Christ with Excerpts from the Life and Works of Its Founder—Bishop C. H. Mason* (Memphis: Church of God in Christ Publishing House, 1969).

17. Mickey Crews, *The Church of God: A Social History* (Knoxville: University of Tennessee Press, 1990), chap. 2.

18. Ibid., chap. 3.

19. Ibid., chap. 5.

20. Synan, *Holiness-Pentecostal*, 162.

21. On the Assemblies of God, there is also a substantial literature. See Grant Wacker, "Assemblies of God," in *Encyclopedia of Religion in*

the South, ed. Samuel S. Hill (Macon, Ga.: Mercer University Press, 1984), 73–75; Margaret M. Poloma, *The Assemblies of God at the Crossroads: Charisma and Institutional Dilemmas* (Knoxville: University of Tennessee Press, 1989); and Blumhofer, *Restoring the Faith,* 116–24.

22. Synan, *Holiness-Pentecostal,* 155–62.

Index

African Americans. *See* Blacks
American Baptist Association, 30, 32.
   See also Landmark Baptists
American Christian Missionary
   Society, 48, 57
Antimission Baptists. *See* Baptists,
   antimission; Primitive Baptists
Antislavery. *See* Slavery
Apostolic Overcoming Holy Church
   of God, 104
Asbury, Francis, 51, 52
Assemblies of God (AOG), 79, 90,
   103–4
Azusa Street Mission, 89, 99–100

Baconian thought, 6, 61, 68, 73
Baptist Missionary Association of
   America, 30, 32. *See also* Landmark
   Baptists
Baptists, 2–12 passim, 15–43, 45,
   82–83, 106–13; antecedents of, 17,
   21, 22, 23, 30; antimission, 2, 26, 28,
   39, 81; Baptistism and, 3, 20, 31;
   black, 2, 12, 20, 33–39, 42, 77, 107,
   109; Calvinism and, 17, 21, 26;

Charleston Tradition of, 16–17, 18,
   19–20, 30; evangelicalism and, 11,
   12, 15, 18, 20, 24, 112; freedom and,
   16, 22, 25, 81; Free Will, 2;
   Fundamentalist, 20, 39–42; Georgia
   Tradition of, 16–17, 18–20; local
   autonomy of, 15–16, 20, 21, 26, 31,
   76, 82–83; Particular, 17; Sandy
   Creek Tradition of, 16–18, 19–20,
   23, 30; Tennessee Tradition of,
   16–17, 19–20. *See also* Black
   churches; Calvinism; Landmark
   Baptists; Primitive Baptists; Sandy
   Creek [N.C.] Church; Separate
   Baptists; Southern Baptist
   Convention
Black churches, 2, 13, 20, 33–39, 65,
   77, 104, 107; denominations of, 20,
   33, 65, 77, 100, 104, 107, 111;
   theology of, 35–39, 77. *See also*
   Blacks; Spirit Movement, blacks
   and
Blacks, 20, 33–34, 65, 66, 75, 77, 99.
   See also Black churches; *and under
   specific groups*

DATE DUE

GAYLORD			PRINTED IN U.S.A.